Praise for *They Did What?*
Unbelievable Tales from the Workplace

Managing escapades, antics, and shenanigans at work aren't for the faint of heart. The narrative format of *They Did What?* brings the stories alive and deepens the readers' understanding of workplace behavior. It applies people management concepts to the gray areas of life.

—Sarah Rajtik, Senior Vice President of Human Resources at American Trucking Associations

If you're in Human Resources, you've likely had an unbelievable workplace experience that made you think, *Somebody should write a book about this! You can't make this stuff up.* Barbara and Cornelia have taken their experiences and the incredible stories of others to craft this delightful book, *They Did What?* In the book, the authors weave a story--based on real stories--of the craziness that happens when working with people. Human Resources professionals will love how Barbara and Cornelia "get" them, and managers and business leaders everywhere will receive comfort in knowing that theirs isn't the only crazy workplace!

—Cathy Fyock, Author, *The Speaker Author* (and former HR professional)

They Did What? is enlightening, entertaining and oh yes, very informative! The only workplace behavior book that I could not put down at 2:00 am!

—**Ann Marie Sabath, Author,** *Everybody Has A Book Inside of Them: How to Bring It Out*

Cornelia and Barbara have written a creative guide filled with valuable information. If you've ever wondered why an employee, peer or boss behaved in such a strange or unfortunate way, this book is for you. The authors take readers on an interesting journey of how people of all types misbehave in organizations and how courageous HR professionals and managers address these issues in a way that helps the organization deal with and move effectively beyond the misbehavior. The insights shared in this book are valuable for managers, leaders, and HR professionals who deal with issues like this on a regular, sometimes daily, basis.

—**Deb Cohen, PhD, Author,** *Developing Management Proficiency*

This book is essential reading for anyone who works with people. You'll be amazed at the stories—especially when you remember they're all based on real-life experiences shared with the authors. I thoroughly enjoyed *They Did What?* and know you will too.

—**Judy Perrault, CEO, Mindbank Consulting Group, LLC**

THEY DID WHAT?

UNBELIEVABLE TALES FROM THE WORKPLACE

OTHER BOOKS BY THESE AUTHORS

Barbara Mitchell & Cornelia Gamlem:

The Big Book of HR

The Essential Workplace Conflict Handbook

The Conflict Resolution Phrase Book

The Manager's Answer Book

Barbara Mitchell & Sharon Armstrong:

The Essential HR Handbook

If you enjoyed this book, or any of our other books, we'd be honored if you'd post a great review on Amazon or Goodreads. Mention something that you really liked about the book(s) and why. The most impactful reviews are short and succinct.

THEY DID WHAT?

UNBELIEVABLE TALES FROM THE WORKPLACE

CORNELIA GAMLEM
BARBARA MITCHELL

They Did What?
Unbelievable Tales from the Workplace

Copyright © 2020 by Cornelia Gamlem & Barbara Mitchell

Paperback ISBN: 978-1-09832-827-6
eBook ISBN: 978-1-09832-828-3

Library of Congress Cataloging-in-Publication Data available upon request.

Printed in the United States of America

To our colleagues and friends
who generously shared their stories with us.

Table of Contents

DISCLAIMER

All HR Professionals have stories to tell. The stories told in this book are composites of situations based on actual events that were told to us by HR and business colleagues. They represent the experiences of a large number of professionals across a wide variety of industries and throughout the course of multiple careers. Likewise, the characters portrayed are a composite of many individuals. We have altered some facts and combined similar stories to protect the privacy of individuals and organizations involved. Nevertheless, these stories are representative of the types of challenges HR professionals face.

Preface

This creative non-fiction book has taken us on quite a journey. During our careers as HR professionals and business leaders, we've met a lot of interesting people. When we decided to write this book—the book all HR professionals threaten to write—we collected stories from our friends and colleagues and used those stories as the basis for this book. However, while many elements of those stories have been fictionalized, the stories you'll read in this book are based on events that really happened.

In order to preserve the privacy and identity of the individuals involved, including our colleagues and the organizations where they worked, we created a fictitious company and cast of characters as a backdrop against which we tell these tales. The characters portrayed are composites of a large number of professionals across a wide variety of industries and throughout multiple careers. It is through all these characters that the stories we tell unfold.

Meet Maryanne Robertson, Chief Human Resources Officer for Kings, a Midwest family restaurant chain, led by CEO Ralph Napoli. Maryanne works closely with Kings' management team as they address the people challenges that occur in any organization. Some of the members of the Leadership Team with recurring roles whom you'll meet include:

- Valerie London, General Counsel;

- Judy Marshall, VP of Food and Beverage;

- Brian Chang, Chief Technology Officer, CTO;

- Bob Zimmerman, Chief Operations Officer, COO; and

- Larry Blackstone, Chief Financial Officer, CFO.

You'll also meet other Kings employees throughout the book, like Tom Horn, Facilities Director, who appears in the first chapter.

Maryanne is supported by a team of talented Human Resources professionals who lead the different HR functions. The ones you'll meet at various times include:

- Kyle Greene, Employee Relations;

- Gloria Lincoln, Employee Benefits;

- Leslie Hernandez, HR Information Systems & Technology;

- Noelle Livingston, Training & Development and

- Ryan Anderson, Administrative Assistant.

She also has a group of peers outside of Kings who meet regularly to exchange ideas and issues and share advice. Be prepared to meet:

- David Morgan, Vice President of HR for a technology firm;

- Stephanie Packard, Director of Compensation & Benefits for a college;

- Ellen Cooper, Vice President of HR for a retail firm;

- Jason Edison, executive coach & consultant; and

- Linda Goodman, executive search.

Since we wanted to write compelling and enticing stories, we worked on our storytelling technique. We realized we had to take the stories we heard, mold them, tweak them, and often combine them to fit the structure of the scenes we created throughout this book. We took real-life situations and put them into realistic settings. The stories you'll read in this book represent composites of the stories we were told. We couldn't make this stuff up.

They Did What? depicts the amazingly difficult challenges and complex issues human resource and business leaders encounter, often daily. And, the situations we describe in these *unbelievable tales* occur more frequently than many readers might suspect. This book is a glimpse into what happens in organizations—often behind the scenes—and how managers and HR professionals deal with the grey areas of work.

CHAPTER 1

The Conference Room Table

Suddenly, I heard Kyle's voice and it brought me back to the present problem. He was trying to explain to a frustrated Tom that these *home-grown stars* of ours couldn't be automatically terminated, today.

Tom turned to me. "Maryanne, um, why would we have to investigate? I don't understand. I mean, they were caught on video. Shouldn't they just be fired?"

"Tom, as Kyle was explaining, we need more information."

"More than we already have? I mean we've got them on video—what more do we need?"

"Well I, for one, haven't seen the video." That made Tom wince.

"Seriously, Tom," I said. "I'm not trying to make you uncomfortable, but we need to know exactly how much, if any, of this escapade was captured on the video, and who else may have had access to it."

* * *

Why did he seem so anxious and edgy on the phone? I thought as I waited for him to arrive. He knows by now we muck around amid shades of grey in this profession. Nothing is ever black and white—straightforward. A sharp knock on the door interrupted my thoughts. "Please come in." The door burst open and in walked Kyle Greene. Then I realized he wasn't alone. Trailing behind was Tom Horn. They were both carrying large mugs filled, I was certain, with strong coffee. This was going to take longer than I expected.

"Kyle, Tom, please sit down," I said motioning to the chairs and table across the room. My full attention was on Kyle, my Employee Relations Manager, and Tom, our Facilities Director as I joined them. Tom seems way too nervous for this to be about an accident or safety incident. Why? He's so easy going and takes things in stride. And Kyle, who is usually so calm, is still so agitated.

"Tom," I said, "what's wrong?" noticing he kept smoothing his tie as if he expected it to take flight. This gave me a clue that he was wanting to get down to whatever brought them here. And Tom usually likes to make small talk. Obviously, this was something out of the ordinary.

Finally, he cleared his throat. "Maryanne, I just told Kyle about something that happened yesterday, and he insisted we bring it right to you so here goes." He stopped and took a sip of coffee. "Yesterday, the Food and Beverage staff had a training session on the new credit card processing procedures in light of all the fraud out there."

What on Earth had happened during a training class that would bring Tom and Kyle to me? As Facilities Director, Tom would not be directly involved with training sessions, except if…. I've been working in human resources long enough to know not to get ahead of the story. Still, I was curious.

"Well, um, when I came in at my usual crack-of-dawn arrival time this morning," Tom said, "the lead IT tech was pacing in front of my door looking about as uncomfortable as I must look right now. Apparently, yesterday's session was live streamed to all the Kings restaurants around the country, and he was monitoring it. He stepped out of the conference room to take a call. When he returned the session was over and people were leaving, so he went back in to turn off the two-way feeds. That's when he noticed two people still in a training room at another site. This isn't unusual—sometimes people stay behind to have a private conversation. But this, well it appeared to be different."

I was confused. Why would IT bring this issue to Tom? Did Brian Chang, our Chief Technology Officer know about it? With that, Kyle jumped in.

"Maryanne, Brian Chang and the IT manager are at a conference and won't be back till tomorrow. The lead tech was concerned there might have been a security breach, and since Security reports to Tom, he told him about the issue this morning."

As he was speaking, I noticed Kyle was moving his neck from side to side as if to relieve some tension.

Now I was even more confused. "Okay, but Tom, what was different about these folks staying behind?"

"Well, um, in this case it was a man and woman who were still in the room. And they, um, weren't having a business conversation. The IT tech overhead her say something about liking it being dangerous and the man, um, said she was being awfully naughty. That's when the IT tech noticed they'd moved to the far end of the table, away from the door, and were standing very close to each other—in what appeared to be an embrace. He wasn't very concerned, yet. He bent over to pick something up and was about to tell them they needed to shut off the computer at their end, when..."

He was silent for a moment, turning his gaze to Kyle, as if looking for reassurance. Kyle took a deep breath, held if for a moment, then blew it out. *His first experience with this issue,* I thought, since I had a sense of what might be coming. He ran his fingers through his slightly long hair—longer than his mother likes—brushing it away from his face and off his collar, before nodding to Tom to continue.

"So, um, when he looked back up, she was sitting on the conference room table with her, um, skirt hiked up around her.... Well, that's when he, um, saw her toss her head back and heard her laugh and, um, say she dared him. Next thing he, um, saw was the man unzipping his pants and reaching in, and, um...well he stopped looking."

"Did he pause the camera or just stop watching?" Kyle said cautiously.

"Kyle, I'm ashamed of you," I laughed to relieve some of the tension. I sensed that both men were uncomfortable talking about sex to me— Tom more so having to describe the particulars—and suspected I might be hearing an abridged version. "And what would your mother think? She did raise you to be a southern gentleman."

Single and 25 years old, Kyle is tall, good looking and has an easy way with people. He can usually find common ground with whomever he meets and is a natural for employee relations. Recently promoted to the position of Employee Relations Manager, I was grooming him to take on more of the issues I'd been dealing with myself. In my role as Chief Human Resources Officer, I needed to spend more time on strategic issues—like workforce planning and employee integration—as Kings

Family Restaurant continues to expand and acquire new restaurants. Just like me, Kyle had worked at Kings—a restaurant chain headquartered in Chicago—as a server during college. Unlike me, who'd explored other industries first, Kyle knew he wanted to work in hospitality and applied for a job at the corporate office as soon as he graduated.

"But seriously," I said, "that's a good question if we have to investigate. Just how much did the tech see, and how much activity was captured?"

Tom told us the technician proceeded to turn off the feed and shut things down. Embarrassed by what he saw, he was fumbling with the equipment. He wasn't sure how much more got recorded, but they needed to preserve the recording for any on-going training needs—folks on vacation, etc. He assured Tom they could edit the last part out.

"Tom, you said this happened yesterday. What time? I'm concerned that he didn't bring this to you or someone until early this morning."

Tom explained that the training session was over at 5:15 pm yesterday. The technician needed to leave right at 5:30 to pick up his kids. He'd secured the camera in the IT safe and no one else except Brian and his manager had access to it. As Tom was talking, my mind drifted to my first encounter with a similar situation.

* * *

Jeri was sitting in the back seat chatting away. "Maryanne, I love that blouse. The color brings out your green eyes, and a great contrast with your dark hair. By the way, Jason, does this stuff really happen at work—people doing the nasty in conference rooms?"

"Uh-huh," Jason had replied.

Our first job out of college was with a large consulting firm, and we were on our way to a client. Jason Edison was the head of HR and accompanied us to provide subject matter expertise for the training our client was rolling out. Jason had a laser focus approach to everything. You could see it in his dark brown eyes, always seemingly fixed in a serious, penetrating gaze—as they were now while he was driving. But if you looked closely, you'd detect a devilish spark in them that revealed his more playful side.

"No joking, how do you deal with this stuff being in HR?" I was stunned that people would actually do this at work.

"Very carefully."

In response, Jeri swept her right hand up in a theatrical gesture and blurted out, "If they were having sex on the table in the conference room, I'll bet the woman was on the bottom. I don't know about you, Maryanne, but I want to be comfortable when I'm having sex. A hard table can't be that comfortable."

A wry grin came over Jason's face as though he had been trying to suppress a laugh. "Jeri, have you been through the sexual harassment training?" He knew Jeri had a passion for the theatre and liked to add a bit of drama to any situation. It made her a good facilitator, but she could get carried away at times.

"Actually, Jeri," he continued, "we shouldn't be joking about this. It could be more serious than you think. And not everyone thinks jokes about sex are funny. Wait till you've both been around awhile. You'll likely be solving conference room table trysts yourselves."

* * *

Suddenly, I heard Kyle's voice and it brought me back to the present problem. He was trying to explain to a frustrated Tom that these *home-grown stars* of ours couldn't be automatically terminated, today.

Tom turned to me. "Maryanne, um, why would we have to investigate? I don't understand. I mean, they were caught on video. Shouldn't they just be fired?"

"Tom, as Kyle was explaining, we need more information."

"More than we already have? I mean we've got the video of them."

"Well I, for one, haven't seen the video." That made Tom wince.

"Seriously, Tom," I said. "I'm not trying to make you uncomfortable, but we need to know exactly how much, if any, of this escapade was captured on the video, and who else may have had access to it.

A teachable moment, I thought as I began to explain to Tom the importance of looking below the surface when making decisions about people's lives and livelihoods. It's not always black and white—it's shades of grey.

"I hadn't thought about that," Tom said.

"There are a number of questions which need answers. Like who else may have been impacted by their conduct besides the IT tech who reported it. Was there an IT tech on their end who might have seen something? Who was responsible for turning off the two-way feed on their end? Were they recording this on their phones? Once we have the full picture and have the issues defined, we can then talk with the respective managers and make recommendations about what needs to happen."

I was so focused on Tom at this point, I was startled when Kyle said, "Maryanne, I think you're forgetting something. Yes, we've got some very reckless behavior to deal with, and the employees' conduct will need to be addressed, but…"

"But what, Kyle?"

"But, ma'am, we don't know *who* did it."

"Kyle, you're absolutely right."

"Well we do know this much," said Tom. "It occurred in one of the restaurants in St. Louis."

"Thanks Tom, that's a start," I said then turned to Kyle. "What do you think we should do first?"

He slowly leaned forward reaching for the pen he'd placed on the table earlier. Picking it up, he replied that we should first lock the camera and the recording in the HR safe and then meet with Judy Marshall, VP of Food and Beverage, to find out the names of the two people involved. Then we needed to get some answers. Are they co-workers or is one on the management team? Have there been issues with either of them in the past? We will need to look at the employee files. We may need to talk with the IT technician. We will have to work with their regional manager and the restaurant's general manager to determine what the appropriate discipline should be. If nothing else, we need to remind people to turn off the camera when the session is over.

I was delighted to hear his plan of action, and it confirmed my instincts about him. Over the past few months, he's realized that in most situations, judgment comes into play when making decisions. He's becoming more skilled at investigating and gathering information and facts.

"I agree that should be our approach, Kyle, so why don't you get the ball rolling with the technology team. I'll contact Judy so she can get the Food and Beverage folks to help us identify these employees. I'll also brief Valerie London. As General Counsel, we may need her help on this."

"Uh, wait," Tom said. "What about the recording? We'll need it for future training."

"The recording will be safe with us for a few days," I continued. "When we do release it, I want to ensure that the same technician who discovered the *activity* does the editing and puts some precautions in place to assure there are no traces of that sensitive material left. We'll need to work with Brian on that part of the process."

I was pleased to see that Tom was a lot more at ease when he left my office then when he'd arrived. Kyle started out the door behind him, but I motioned for him to stay.

"Let's get Ryan in here to coordinate the sequence of our meetings and phone discussions." Ryan Anderson was my assistant, but much more. A recent college graduate with a degree in HR, he is a computer whiz, great at social media, and has interest in learning whatever the team wants to share with him. He helps everyone with scheduling, reports, and whatever else is needed to keep a busy department operating.

We spent another hour going over our strategy for the investigation while Ryan set up our meetings and phone calls. He'd learned quickly from Kyle how to discreetly *invite* people into discussions with us. We knew we'd have to act quickly since we didn't want any of this to go viral. At one point, Kyle asked, "Do people even think? Actions have consequences and this one action is going to be embarrassing and potentially damaging to two people's jobs. There are days when I wish I didn't have to work with people but then, guess I wouldn't have a job if it weren't for our employees."

I shifted in my chair. "Kyle, would you rather be working in another area of human resources?"

He started to laugh. "Relax, Maryanne. I'm not going anywhere. A friend keeps telling me I should get into recruiting, but I enjoy employee relations. I like the uncertainty. You never know what's going to come through the door."

I could still hear Jason saying all those years ago, "Wait till you've been around awhile." I smiled at Kyle and said, "Maybe we can use this in some way to talk about consequences of bad behavior and make something positive out of this. You know, my grandmother always said that people make you tired. She was right." As I pushed my chair back to stand up, I noticed that the room had grown darker. I glanced outside and realized the sky was cloudy. I sighed. *Before long, I'll be looking at a grey winter sky and all the challenges a Chicago winter brings. For now, Kyle and I will have to deal with this latest issue and the challenge of managing in the grey area.*

CHAPTER 2

Misery Loves Company

"Speaking of sex on the company furniture," Jason said, "Maryanne, do you remember your first time?"

Raising an eyebrow, I heard myself saying, "Excuse me!" before Jason could say anything else.

As everyone burst into laughter, a blushing Jason said, "Let me explain. We were doing training for a client's night shift employees. Rumor had it that two nights earlier the supervisor heard noises inside the conference room reserved for the training. So, he unlocked the door. To his disbelief, he found a half-naked couple having sex on the conference room table. Their slacks and underwear were laying in a pile on the floor along with a condom wrapper. In their haste to get dressed and leave, she left her panties behind. We heard he sent them home that night and both were fired the next day."

"Oh, so the noises he heard were panting and groaning?" Ellen Cooper quipped. "But I wonder why they fired them right away. That seems pretty impulsive. Why not take disciplinary action?"

"Good point, Ellen," Jason said sitting straighter in his chair. "There was a lot we didn't know as consultants. We didn't know the client's policies. We didn't know these people's histories. We didn't know if there were other issues with them."

Today's my day to host the peer networking group of HR Executives who work in different industries. We support each other by sharing problems and offering solutions. Having trusted colleagues outside the organization to help with issues is a privilege. Having the benefit of their knowledge, objectivity, and confidentiality is a great advantage. Since we all recognize the seriousness of many workplace situations *and* the absurdity of some situations that people put themselves into, we serve as sounding boards for each other. At times we just have to laugh at those ludicrous situations with colleagues who understand. We couldn't survive in a job like this without each other and the ability to let off steam in a totally safe environment.

I'd just finished telling the group about the escapade of the employees having sex in the conference room and it being recorded—wondering whose story was going to top it. I knew this was a topic that would spark some great, if not raucous, memories and Jason Edison was quick to recall one of ours. He and I met when we both worked for the same consulting firm—my first job out of college. Ten years ago, he became certified as a master coach and started a coaching and consulting practice with a colleague.

David Morgan didn't waste any time. "Maryanne, I feel your pain and yes, been there—done that!" As we all broke into laughter, he stopped himself, "C'mon. You know I didn't mean I've done the nasty on the conference room table. I meant I've had to deal with similar situations."

David's a smart, opinionated, funny, and generous man who loves to bring new challenges to the group, then sit back and watch the sparks fly. I just knew we were in for an interesting meeting.

"A year or so ago, I got a panic call around 11 pm from a manager who was working late. You know how techies operate—we have people in the building 24/7. In fact, I'm concerned some of them actually live there, but that's another issue altogether. Well, imagine my surprise when the manager said he'd gone outside to get something from his car and saw a group of people standing outside a first-floor conference room window staring in, laughing, and snickering. He had no idea what they were looking at, but as he approached, he realized you could see inside through the window and everyone was watching two people going at it on the conference room table. Seems the group was outside taking a smoke break when one of them spotted something interesting in the window. He called the others over to watch. Who knows how long they'd been out there enjoying a pretty X-rated show. The manager herded everyone back inside. He really had to work hard to convince them to give up the entertainment—no one wanted to leave. Then he debated what to do next. He knew he had to stop the situation inside but wasn't sure who was involved. So, he went to the conference room and made a lot of noise before opening the door. He found the couple rushing to put their clothes back on. He was shocked to see one of the guilty parties—a highly respected VP. Obviously, he wasn't using good judgment that night. We had no idea the conference room was visible from outside at night."

David is the Vice President of HR for a technology company in Naperville, a western suburb of Chicago, and I met him when we were on a panel together a few years ago. The thing about David is that while he has a great sense of humor, he takes employee issues very seriously and approaches each one in a very deliberate manner. That's why he suggested starting this networking group, so we could share perspectives. I am forever grateful to him for doing so. Heading up the human resources function can be a lonely job at times, and I always learn something when we meet.

The sides of Ellen's mouth turned up. "What did you do when the manager shared this bombshell, David? Ask for a detailed description of what he saw through the conference room window?"

"No. C'mon. The next night, I called them both in and told them what had been observed. They couldn't deny it. We put them on unpaid leave while we investigated. Turns out the woman involved worked directly for the VP. As part of the management team, he was held to a higher standard of behavior, so we terminated him for violating those standards and our trust. Not to mention exercising incredibly poor judgment. She, on the other hand, was given a strong warning since it was her first offense. And, you can bet we had the maintenance staff replace the conference room windows with something that couldn't been seen through at any time of the day or night."

I looked around the room and saw some uneasy smiles. "David, somehow I don't think the story ended there."

"Maryanne, you never cease to amaze me with your mind-reading ability. And can you teach me how do you do it? It's a great skill for a CHRO to have."

He went on to share that the terminated VP's wife had stormed into his office the next day and demanded the woman be fired too. She claimed the woman had pursued her poor husband, and he was an innocent victim who shouldn't have been fired. And she had proof—emails and notes the woman had sent her husband—proof she wasn't afraid to take to the press.

Ellen and I exchanged incredulous looks before I said, "She was defending him? Did you read any of the emails? I'm surprised she didn't just dump the guy."

David told us they got their outside attorneys and their PR department involved. The emails and notes were vague, and the woman was furious when questioned about it. She said she didn't want anything else to do with the company but wouldn't leave without a package—compensation and outplacement help. Apparently, that's what they did, and there was no adverse effect for the firm. He had no idea what happened to the marriage or, for that matter, the relationship between the former VP and the woman involved. It just wasn't their business once it was resolved legally.

"Well *I'd* want to know but then again, I've never had to deal with one of these situations," said Ellen, "but, I bet I can top it. How about sex in the walk-in cooler? Brad, my significant other, encountered that when he worked for a fast food company during college—don't worry, Maryanne, not Kings—not that I would consider Kings fast food but just in case you were worried, it wasn't your company!"

"Thanks for clarifying," I laughed. "Go on, this sounds like something we want to hear."

Ellen is the newest member of the group. She met David at an HR tech conference, and he invited her to join the group. She heads up HR for a start-up retail company and has one of the most analytical minds of anyone I know. She is passionate about understanding how data impacts the HR function. That's why our discussions at these networking meetings challenge her in a positive way. Employee behavior can't be quantified.

"It seems Brad needed cheese for the line," she continued, "so he went into the walk-in cooler. There was his manager and one of the line cooks—stark naked and having sex. Right there. In the cooler. Among the produce, cheese, meat, whatever. Looking down and away from the scene, Brad backed out as quickly and quietly as he could. But not before his manager caught his eye. As he left, she shook her head as if to say, don't tell anyone."

"Were they so hot they needed a place to cool off?" quipped David as he brushed a stray hair off his blue, button-down shirt. "And what did Brad do? Did he run out and never return? Seriously, what a difficult position to be in as a young employee in that kind of operation. I might have done just that—run away—at that point in my working career."

"No, but the story didn't stop there," said Ellen. "Once she emerged from the freezer, the manager pulled Brad aside and told him he'd better not say anything about this, or else. Brad felt she was a bit of a bully, and these events made him uncomfortable. He even suspected she might hit on him. Or worse, expect him to engage in the same activity. So, he talked it over with his parents first. His dad suggested he contact the corporate HR department where he had gone for his new employee orientation. This took a lot of guts, but he called and made an appointment. The next night at work—his appointment was the following day—his manager called him into the office. She told him if he kept this to himself, she'd make it worth his while. He was totally disgusted at this point. He didn't say anything to her, kept his appointment, and quit shortly after that. He heard that the manager was not fired but was transferred to another store and nothing happened to the man in question. He never ate at that restaurant again—couldn't get the picture of naked people rolling around on the cooler floor surrounded by raw burgers out of his mind."

David turned in his chair and stared seriously at Ellen. "Is Brad still in therapy over this?"

While everyone was laughing, Jason leaned back in his chair. He was always thoughtful about the words he chose, and I could tell he was getting ready to make a point. "This is why our work is so complicated. I certainly think I would have fired the manager for her actions, but who knows what was going on in the background. Maybe she was the daughter of the owner or the person with those blackmail pictures from the holiday party we all joke about."

"Good reminder," I said. "We make decisions along with our managers, and those decisions impact everyone—well beyond the people who cause the problems in the first place. But our profession's like an iceberg. People only see what's above the surface. What's visible. They don't see ninety percent of what we do—the stuff that occurs below the surface and behind the scenes.

"So true," chimed in Stephanie Packard. "And we can't forget that good people want to work with other good people. Which reminds me. We had a messy one at the college recently. There are several employees on the grounds crew who sometimes work at night on projects that can't be done when students were walking all over campus. Y'know, repairing sidewalks, taking out diseased trees, things like that. To our shame, they aren't always supervised. Well, this one couple apparently likes to sneak off during their shift—and be gone for long stretches of time—assuming their co-workers would pick up the slack. One night someone on the crew who was tired of covering for them, suspected what they were doing. So, he followed them to the parking lot. He saw them get into a car. He waited a few minutes before moving closer. There they were in the car, and they weren't talking. They were heavily engaged in their sexual activity, so much so they didn't hear him approach. So, he snapped a picture. It was dark and the picture didn't reveal too much detail—but it was enough for him to prove they weren't working."

Stephanie is my dear friend and mentor. Tall, with a warm and welcoming personality, she might remind you of your favorite aunt. But that doesn't stop her from taking a very objective view of situations, which likely comes from her finance background. She and I hit it off immediately when we met several years ago. The oldest person in the group at 62, she's currently the compensation and benefits director at a local community college. She started her career in banking and transitioned into HR when she realized she really enjoyed solving problems involving people and not just numbers. With her background, it was no wonder she found a career in human resources designing complex compensation and total rewards programs.

"Wait, Stephanie," said Ellen. "What did these two love birds do when the picture was taken. No reaction?"

"They were otherwise occupied at the time," said Stephanie. "The next day the coworker went to their manager and told what was going on. He forwarded the manager the picture. Both were confronted and questioned individually. And shocked that they'd been caught. They didn't deny anything but did try to justify it saying they had nowhere else to go to be together. They were *in love* but married to other people! Our investigation showed they hadn't been doing good work for quite some time. And they'd been signing in and out for each other—a work rule requiring immediate dismissal. So, we terminated them both, and we put their supervisor on a disciplinary notice since he wasn't managing his people to our standards."

"Sounds more like they were *in lust*," said Ellen.

Jason leaned back in his chair smiling. "Looks like we've all had this issue one time or another. I once faced an *in lust* moment during a corporate retreat—complete with cocktail hour followed by dinner which was accompanied by a lot of wine. After dinner, some people went to the lounge continuing to drink. As the evening wore on and people left to go to their rooms, one man and one woman remained behind. Both were single and peers, so no reporting relationship issue. But they'd apparently been attracted to each other for a while and decided that night was the night to do something about it. Well, you can imagine, or maybe you can't—but I have to admit I was shocked when I heard they decided to have sex on the pool table right there in the lounge, in a public setting, where anyone could have come in and seen them. And unfortunately for them, someone did see them—one of the partners who'd come down to the lounge for a quiet night cap."

We all were laughing at the mental image Jason had painted for us but knew it really wasn't funny. "Not only did the company have to pay for the damage to the pool table," he continued, "but we had to meet with the two employees. They were mortified and very apologetic and promised not to do anything like this in the future. Since there wasn't really any issue about their relationship that impacted the company, we had them pay for the damage and placed a disciplinary notice in each of their employee files. They turned out to be model employees and, in fact, both made partner years later. So, the story had a good ending."

"It's interesting that these similar situations are handled differently in different organizations," said Stephanie. "That's the hardest thing to get across to the younger staff and sometimes to managers. There isn't one magic answer or solution that works all the time. So much depends on the circumstances, the culture and environment of the organization, and the employees' track records and histories."

"You mentioned making impulsive decisions earlier, Ellen," I said. "In the training room situation I told you about, Tom, the facilities director, wanted to know why we didn't jump right to termination based on our code of conduct. I had to reel him back and remind him to look at all of the facts, the big picture."

"You never did tell us what finally happened to those two employees involved," said Ellen.

"Both worked in St. Louis. He was an assistant shift manager. She was an accounting specialist in the regional office and sometimes filled in as a hostess at his restaurant. There'd been some reports of suspicious behavior by them in the past, but nothing conclusive. There was the time they both came up from the supply room looking disheveled—and she had no reason to be down there. And the time they were caught in his office with the lights out—she appeared to be buttoning her top. There were a few other similar observations. Apparently, discretion was not a value for either of them. She had a good record in accounting, but he was only mediocre as a shift manager. The recording showed as they were finishing up in the training room, they were making plans for their next tryst in the restaurant the coming weekend. He said something like 'this is going to be hard to beat.' Her response was something crude. When confronted, they both admitted this was a sort of game for them. They didn't see each other outside of work. The decision to terminate them both was made pretty easily after reviewing all the evidence."

"What ever happened with the recording? And did you ever discover if they were recording it on their phones?" laughed Ellen.

"The IT tech involved was able to edit the nasty parts out, so we had a version to use for training. The original is being retained in our general counsel's office. And no, they weren't recording it. In fact, they were unaware the camera was still running. We got the impression they were a little excited to find out their dangerous activity was memorialized."

Ellen wiggled her eyebrows. "Maybe they'll start their own X-rated YouTube channel."

"As long as Kings isn't the sponsor, right, Maryanne?" said David, with a grin.

As she picked up her reading glasses from the table, Stephanie said, "That's probably enough dramady for me for one night." It was our cue to wrap things up for the evening.

I was thinking how these meetings energize me. "You're right, Stephanie. As always, I'm energized and exhausted by our discussions, but I appreciate each of you and can't wait till our next meeting. By the way, who's hosting next month?"

"That would be me," said David as he waved goodbye and headed out.

CHAPTER 3

Bad Bosses

"The entire kitchen crew—every last one of them is threatening to walk out during the breakfast rush. You've got to get right over to the Loop restaurant and help me right now." Rob Wiley, the District Manager for Kings Family Restaurants' Midwest district, was my first call of the day and absolutely not one I expected. Rob is usually a really together kind of a guy, so I assured him I would be there as soon as I could get a cab. I called Kyle Greene, our Employee Relations Manager, and asked him to get me the current list of the kitchen crew at that restaurant then meet me in the elevator lobby so we could immediately head to the State Street restaurant.

When you're in charge of the human resources function for a regional restaurant chain with over 100 restaurants, no day is ever the same as the day before or what you planned for, and trust me, I couldn't have imagined what this day would bring.

The State Street restaurant is the flagship for Kings Family Restaurants. It was the first location Ralph Napoli's—our CEO—family opened back in the 40's after his father returned from World War II where he'd been a cook. We continue to serve some of the family recipes brought over from Italy, and those were now usually the widely popular daily specials. In fact, Ralph was considering making some major changes in the menu to feature more of his family recipes to set us apart from the competition. Menu changes, including the possibility of introducing the farm to table concept, are a topic on today's Leadership Team meeting agenda. Unless this crisis gets out of control, I want to be back in time for the meeting because I strongly support Ralph's ideas but know others aren't yet convinced.

Kyle was waiting for me in the lobby and said he'd emailed the kitchen crew list to me. I was grateful for my quick-thinking team. Kyle had a cab waiting for us. We jumped in, and I shared what I'd heard from Rob.

The trip to the restaurant was quick and as I got out of the cab, I noticed people who I assumed were potential customers coming out the door. They didn't look happy. One man came storming out and almost knocked someone down. As he brushed passed me, I heard him muttering something, but couldn't understand what he was saying. It didn't sound like anything favorable.

Rob was waiting for us outside the restaurant and quickly filled us in. "This is really bad. Now it has expanded beyond the kitchen crew. Every single employee is upset, but no one will tell me what's going on. The cooks are standing around with arms folded, the servers are huddled near the break room—you can feel the tension building. I've tried everything I can think of to get them to talk to me, but they won't. Maryanne, I need your good people skills to get to the bottom of this. We've got a room full of hungry customers and a line at the coffee bar waiting for takeout."

As we walked in, I saw nearly every table was full. This is a prime location for busy office workers to catch breakfast on their way in to work. But I didn't see any food on the tables—not a good sign. I asked Rob where Archie, the manager, was. An uncomfortable look came over his face. "I sent him to the produce market. I have a feeling he's the problem, so I wanted him out of the way."

Kyle was craning his neck to look at the take-out line where most of the customers where looking down at their smartphones—many with their thumbs rapidly moving. Kyle whispered that he'd check Twitter and if needed, alert the social media staff in PR. Good point I thought. Here's another reason having a diverse team makes sense. While I am as social media savvy as a 40-something mother of teenage twins can be, Kyle is younger and more attuned to how quickly things can spiral out of control in the world of instant news.

I took a deep breath and we went directly to the kitchen. As I looked around, I was shocked to see the entire staff was standing right inside the door. They were either frowning or looked hostile and very few made eye contact. And I didn't see any eggs on the grill or smell bacon cooking.

As I introduced myself, I looked around the room and saw many long-time Kings' employees who knew me. What was more important, I knew them and their commitment to the Napoli family and Ralph in particular. I needed to find out as quickly as possible what had caused this mass frustration, but the first order of business was to get them back to work. We had customers to feed, and Kings is all about the customer experience.

Trying not to show my concern, I smiled. "Good morning. I understand something has upset you to the point you've said you are all quitting today, but I am asking you to give us a chance to work it out. I promise as soon as the morning rush is over, we'll sit down with each of you to get to the bottom of this. Many of you know me and I think know I'm an honorable person who will keep my word. For those who don't know me, I'm Maryanne Robertson, and I head up the human resources department at Kings. I've worked at Kings for over 15 years and actually worked as a server at the Evanston Kings when I was in college, so I know a little about what you do. I can't promise anything more right now than listening to what's upsetting you, but please, will you help us feed the valued customers who are here now waiting for their breakfast?"

I watched the employee's faces as they listened intently to me, but I could tell they were not happy. As I looked at each employee, I saw a few eye rolls, but I also saw some slight nods. Several of the long-term employees wouldn't meet my gaze which really concerned me.

Kyle was making his way through where the servers were standing. He has such a great way with people, and I noticed a few people giving him slight smiles. He is such a charmer—I think some of the women couldn't help but respond to him. Finally, one of the line cooks who had been there the longest said, "I can't let the customers down. I will go back to work but will hold you to the promise you just made us. You said that you'll listen to what we have to say." He turned to his co-workers. "She's always been fair with us, so how about it? Let's go to work and deal with our problems after the morning rush."

The rest of the kitchen crew nodded their agreement, and I smiled my thanks at them as they put on their aprons and hats and returned to their appointed tasks. Rob took over managing the kitchen, and I asked him to send each person out to us one by one when he could spare them.

That was the easy part—now I had to make good on my promise to listen and get to the root of their issues. Kyle and I went out to the restaurant, grabbed coffee pots, and made the rounds filling up cups and thanking the customers for their patience. We let them know we were back on track and they'd get their breakfast soon. As soon as we saw food beginning to arrive on tables, we made our way to a corner booth away from most of the customers. As I sat down and reached for my coffee Kyle asked, "What could be going on? It has to be something really big to get the entire staff upset like this."

"We'll figure this out quickly if we listen carefully." Just then I noticed the line cook who'd been instrumental in calming the troops coming towards us. I welcomed him, introduced Kyle, and sat back to hear what was going on.

It didn't take long at all. After talking with a handful of the kitchen staff, we knew we had a problem and the problem was Archie, the manager. We were getting the picture after the third person told of how their schedules had been unpredictable for months. Sometimes Archie wouldn't post the weekly schedule until late on Sunday night so no one could plan their week. One of the servers broke down in tears as she told us how difficult it was to arrange day care when she didn't know from week to week when she'd be on the schedule. She said she'd been paying a penalty for being late to pick up her kids which was negatively impacting her financial situation.

One of the great things about Kings is we recognize and reward our people for great work and loyal service. Employees are encouraged to wear their service award pins on their aprons, so we very quickly realized we were talking with people who'd been loyal employees for years. One woman who was wearing a 20-year pin told me, with tears in her eyes, her husband had just gone on disability. She lives in fear of losing her job if she does something Archie doesn't like. She said she'd even thought about quitting but loves her customers at Kings—and where would she go at her age anyway? I had to hold back my own tears at this point but knew I had to stay objective.

For a while I was thinking this wouldn't be hard to resolve. We'd need Archie to focus more on a firm schedule, so people could plan their lives. I started to relax, but unfortunately, things moved downhill fast as new issues were uncovered.

Several of the staff shared stories of feeling disrespected personally along with stories they'd heard of Archie muttering racial slurs under his breath and bullying some of the new staff members who were primarily from South American countries. We heard numerous complaints of him using rough language and, while that wasn't unusual in kitchens, he seemed to have crossed the line. One of the cooks told me he felt like he'd been singled out when Archie called him names—names he was too embarrassed to share with me. Kyle offered to talk with him privately so his concerns could be shared, and the cook agreed. Finally, we heard Archie persisted in teasing one particular employee about his sexual orientation.

The staff felt unappreciated and diminished, and they were really unhappy. We knew what we were dealing with when several of the employees said basically the same thing, "I love my job and the company, and so admire Mr. Napoli and what he stands for, but my manager is a jerk."

Once the breakfast rush was over, Kyle and I sat down with Rob and shared what we'd learned. We had loyal employees who weren't being treated with the dignity they deserved, and Rob had a manager who wasn't living up to our company's values. We also had a potential issue with discrimination, and we needed to head it off quickly.

Rob called Archie and told him not to come back to the restaurant but to meet us at my office at 4 pm. Then, he and I met with the employees, told them we'd heard their concerns, and advised Rob would be filling in as manager until we resolved the issue. A cheer went up as the employees high fived each other. We also thanked them for bringing this to our attention and asked them not to be so dramatic next time they were unhappy. Threatening to walk out—especially on customers—wasn't acceptable. I agreed to meet with Rob at 3 pm to plan what we would say to Archie. Rob took off his suit jacket, loosened his tie, put his apron back on and went into the kitchen to get the crew started on prep for lunch.

Kyle and I raced back to the office—this time on foot—and I barely had time to check in with Judy Marshall, our VP of Food and Beverage and Rob's boss, and brief her before we both headed to the conference room for the Leadership Team meeting. Judy is a trusted colleague, and we have bonded over being female in a male-dominated industry. She's shared what a struggle it's been for her to be taken seriously. Almost six feet tall and model thin, she is a stunning African American woman. She can be a bit abrasive at times, but she has an amazing drive for doing good work and constant improvement. I'm sure that is why Ralph respects her so much.

Looking over the lunch buffet on the corner table, I helped myself to a delicious looking spinach salad and a warm roll and butter, while eyeing the sandwiches and a fruit salad. How nice it is to work for a restaurant company. I couldn't help noticing a plate of cream cheese frosted brownies and oatmeal cookies at the end of the line, but I avoided taking one—on my way out, perhaps, but not yet.

As we gathered around the conference table, I was struck again by how much I enjoyed working with this team. Yes, there were sometimes disagreements and we frequently had passionate discussions, but we all respected each other which made for a strong team. Ralph is a great leader. He grew up in the hospitality business and has good instincts about how to get the best from his people. When I'd worked for Kings during college, I had met him a couple of times when he visited our restaurant. He'd always come in with a smile and something positive to say. He was totally observant. I was amazed at the small details he could spot in a restaurant. One of the many examples I'd seen was when he came into the kitchen when I was picking up an order and told the cook he was using too much cheese on the chopped salad which could over power the taste. He could tell just by looking at the finished product. The cook wasn't offended because Ralph told him in a non-confrontational way. So, when I decided to leave the consulting firm I joined right out of college, going to work for Ralph seemed like the logical thing to do. However, I couldn't help but think about some of the not so great bosses I've had along the way. And while I'll admit I learned from those bosses, I much prefer to learn from a strong, reasonable manager whom I can respect.

Ralph has the genuine ability to make you feel as if you are the only person in the room, even when it's a room filled with people. He has a warm smile and eyes that sparkle when he laughs, which is often. In fact, I think his sense of humor is one of his best leadership qualities. He is a master at putting people at ease and when people are relaxed, I think they do their best work. And that's why working for Ralph is such a joy.

I wish I could say the same about my first boss at the consulting firm. Working there right out of college was a great way to start in my career in business, and I learned so much from a variety of clients. But my first boss was more than difficult to work for. He was a liar and a cheat, and he was lazy. He bragged about padding his expense reports by having his wife drive him to the airport, but submitting forged receipts for cab rides, or ordering two entrees when on travel because *the company owes me for all the work I do.* He laughed about taking his dirty shirts with him on business trips, putting them into the hotel laundry, then charging the company. The little time he spent in the office was behind closed doors with instructions he wasn't to be disturbed. Yet his staff worked hard and never complained.

I was an idealistic newcomer to the business world, and this just didn't feel right. So, I contacted Ralph to see if there might be a job open at Kings, and it was a smart decision.

Ralph came into the room ending my trip down memory lane. At the start of these meetings, we each typically take a few minutes to share what is going on in our particular area of the business, quickly getting our issue out. If there is something needing everyone's input, that person gets to go first so there is enough time to resolve the issue. Today, I started and shared what had happened at the Loop restaurant location this morning.

Since Judy was up to speed, she quickly spoke up, saying she was committed to quick, appropriate action to resolve the issues uncovered that morning. Her first reaction was to fire Archie, but I suggested we needed to look at any documentation we might have on his performance and talk to him before we made a decision. Ralph and the rest of the Leadership Team were in agreement.

I thought we'd move on to the next agenda item, but it seemed like everyone around the table wanted to share their experiences with incompetent bosses. Ralph stepped in and did what he usually does and asked people to go in turn. Valerie London, our General Counsel lost no time in speaking up.

Valerie's strength comes from her ability to quickly capture the essence of any discussion or situation, and then articulate a clear plan of action. She has a no-nonsense approach to dealing with employee and business issues, and she and I work extremely well together. I was surprised to hear her jump in with a story she never shared with me before—and she's shared many.

"Early in my career, I was staff attorney at a tech firm. We had a manager who took the cake—except he didn't eat cake. He'd brag about getting up at 4 am every day to work out and complain that the staff didn't do the same, not caring they had other priorities. He'd say, 'If I have time, so should you.' To make it worse, he dressed like he was on the cover of GQ and expected the rest of his team to do the same. You know what it's like in the tech culture—most days you're lucky if your staff comes in with shoes and a tee shirt and only hope the writing on the shirt isn't too obscene. But, to expect everyone would dress like he did was a bit much. Worst of all he was lazy, pretty incompetent, and very competitive with all his peers. He would tell his number two person almost daily, 'just make me look good,' and not to help other VPs with their projects—that her job was 'to make him look good.' That was the day she decided to leave, and it was a big loss. Although I didn't have much to do with him, he's been my negative role model ever since. I never want to act like he did."

Bob Zimmerman, our COO, who usually is quiet in our meetings when Ralph is present, was flipping his pen from side to side. When we hired him, some of the team thought he was just being deferential to Ralph and questioned whether he could be effective in the COO role. We soon realized that he is a great listener and a highly strategic thinker. We underestimated Bob so I was very interested when he asked, "May I share a situation I observed in our industry years ago? I worked with a kitchen manager—probably a lot like Archie—who picked on anyone he thought was weak and dealt with guys in the kitchen by calling them *queer* or *gay*. Most of the time people just laughed it off, thinking it was his way of blowing off steam till one day when we lost a great employee over it, someone who just couldn't take it anymore and confronted the manager. He said he wasn't gay but even if he was, he didn't like the way the manager handled his staff in the kitchen, and he quit. We learned some painful lessons—that good employees are hard to find and that how people are treated can make a huge difference in results. That's when we started our communications training to help employees and especially managers work more productively. Had to get the message out that our business is based on providing outstanding customer service and that begins with how well they work with each other."

I almost fell out of my chair. Bob has never been a fan of things that cost the organization money—like management training or employee development. I filed this comment away for the future. I was sure it would come in handy someday when Bob suggested cutting my employee development budget.

Judy turned to Bob, tilting her head back. "It is amazing any of us survive early work experiences. My favorite is when I had a manager who would come in every morning and gather us all around the kitchen island and tell us what our specials would be that day. We soon learned he just made stuff up and hadn't talked with the executive chef or with purchasing to see what products we had to work with. Before we caught on that he wasn't mentally stable, we'd get started working on what we could to make the specials he'd asked for, but before we finished, he'd come in and say, 'Why are you making that? I didn't ask you for that.' It was as if he didn't remember telling us his plan for the day. Once we realized it, we'd just pretend to listen, nod when he shared his plans, and then go on with the actual menu the executive chef had prepared. Of course, we wondered why he had this great job since he didn't seem to understand our business. Then we found out his wife was the owner's daughter. That explained it all. It didn't make it any easier to deal with on a daily basis, but at least we knew why he had the job and we needed to make him happy. And it was the reason I left that restaurant."

Ralph looked up from his iPad where we knew he kept the meeting agenda, and said, "Judy, that is a good reminder of why we pay attention to how our managers are selected and trained. We sure don't want a poor manager to cause us to lose our good employees." Another reason to love Ralph, I thought.

"Ever have a boss who cried all the time?" said Brian Chang, our Chief Technology Officer and the youngest member of our Leadership Team. We all whipped our heads around to see him with a huge grin on his face. "She cried all the time. She'd call me into her office and start telling me all her problems at work and at home and cry. And, I don't mean she'd get tears in her eyes—I mean she would sob like her heart was breaking. The issues she was sharing with me were not doom-and-gloom—I mean, no one was dying or even close to it. Sometimes, she'd cry in our staff meetings for no apparent reason and no one knew what to do. Once, someone tried to comfort her, but she motioned her away. After that, we'd all look at each other and shrug our shoulders. There were times when we all just got up and left the room so she could get herself together. She never apologized or mentioned it, so we guessed it really didn't bother her. I was so happy when I got promoted out of her department. I guess she's still there and probably still crying."

Brian is very creative and innovative. I'm constantly encouraging Ralph to keep him challenged especially at a time we're trying to leverage the newest technologies. Despite his youth, Brian has a great deal of business acumen and can make a solid business case, complete with a cost-benefit analysis, to Ralph and Larry Blackstone, our Chief Financial Officer, who is generally resistant to any changes that come with a large price tag.

Ralph let the stories continue for a while before saying, "What we've just been discussing is a vivid reminder of why we focus our attention and our management development programs on the right way to manage people. I hope you've all learned something today." Then he pulled us back to the task at hand. He asked me what Rob and I planned to do when we met with Archie. He very emphatically said under no circumstances should anyone at Kings behave the way Archie had been behaving. During the meeting, Kyle texted me to say he'd found nothing negative Archie's employee file. In fact, Archie had a satisfactory rating on his last performance appraisal. He'd been thought of as a high performer which was why he had been moved recently to the flagship location—a plum assignment where good performers get noticed. I shared this with the Leadership Team and watched as people around the table got the message that this wasn't good news.

I looked at Rob's boss, Judy, who nodded sheepishly. "I know, Maryanne. This is a great example of what you're always advising us to do—document. Who knows, maybe he's been behaving like this for a long time and it's been overlooked and now we have a mess on our hands. I'll meet with you and Rob this afternoon to put a performance plan together for Archie and we'll either see a quick turnaround or we'll follow our policy toward termination. I'm thinking we should move Archie to another location so Rob can closely monitor him and put someone new in the Loop restaurant, at least in the short term. And we need to let all the employees understand how committed we are to treating all our employees with respect. This may take a few meetings and some one-on-ones so I may be calling on some of you to help. The staff needs to know the Leadership Team totally supports this action and reinforces our commitment to them and to the other great employees we depend on."

Ralph wanted to know if there was any other fallout from the incident. Brian said the IT team was searching social media for any negative comments about the company posted this morning. We all noticed Ralph sitting up straighter in his chair and leaning forward. Before he could say anything, Brian assured him the comments they'd uncovered weren't too damaging.

"We've forwarded them to public relations, and they are looking them over right now, Ralph. They'll let us know their assessment this afternoon. My guess is they'll recommend doing nothing at this time."

"Thanks, Brian," said Ralph. "Just keep me informed. Folks, I think we've had enough excitement for today. Let's adjourn."

Later that afternoon, we met with Archie, but everything we'd planned went out the window. He came into my office, saw Rob and Judy, and the look on his face said it all. Before I could even speak, he said, "I've had it with you people and how you baby your employees. The restaurant world is a tough business and if you don't know that, you're in the wrong profession." Then he stormed out, slamming the door behind him.

Rob, Judy, and I agreed that he should be terminated immediately and when I ran it by Ralph, he said with a deep frown, "I agree, he needs to go—now. His management style is seriously flawed and totally contrary to our mission. I'm less concerned about his comments about us than I am about what you heard from our employees—let's move him out of the organization and do it now."

Valerie and I agreed to put a termination package together and have it ready the next day. Archie's behavior was so not the *Kings Way*.

After a day like this one, I realized again how fortunate I am to work with such great leaders who don't run away from challenging situations. Then, it flashed in my mind that we'd never discussed the farm to table menu ideas—another day and time.

I was delighted to get out of the office and home for dinner which Jack, my husband, had ordered from the local pizza place. After a fun night with my family, I followed up on emails and saw I had several from employees at the Loop restaurant thanking me for listening to them today. That felt really good. I hoped they'd understand we always had their backs.

CHAPTER 4

Is This Your Penis?

Unbelievable doesn't begin to describe it. I've done this so many times, but I couldn't have predicted what I heard this particular night. Frequently I speak at local colleges about HR issues, and I always enjoy the interaction with people who are preparing for a career. This night was…well, I already said it…it was more than unbelievable.

Tonight, as I finished my presentation, I did what I usually did before I stepped down from the stage and asked the audience to share their best stories with me, either now or later by email or text. There was a line of people wanting to talk to me, but I noticed something unusual. A young woman was sort of hanging back as if she wanted to be the last person I met that night—as if she had something more on her mind than thanking me for my presentation.

Finally, it was her turn and she introduced herself as Bella. "Since we both work in the hospitality field, I have a story to share that I just wasn't comfortable sharing with the others. I'm new to my organization and, even if I changed all the names, I'm afraid it might get me in trouble with my management. Do you have a few minutes now?"

I glanced at my phone and saw it wasn't that late. I only had two texts, one from each of my daughters and neither said the house was on fire or anything else life threatening, so I said, "Yes." We sat down in the front row of seats in the now empty auditorium. She wasn't wearing her nametag, and I assumed she removed it before she decided to stick around. Later I knew why she was keeping her organization private.

Bella said she was a recent graduate from this university where she'd earned a business degree with a concentration in human resources. I congratulated her on her achievement commenting on her decision to study both business and HR. "Had she found a job yet?" I asked thinking if she was undecided, she might be a good candidate for our management training program at Kings.

"I have, with one of the big Chicago downtown hotels. I'm the HR Assistant Manager. I thought it would be a great way to learn all the many roles HR plays in an organization. And, something happened recently I think might go on your top HR stories list."

That got my attention. What could this young woman have experienced so early in her HR career? I leaned forward to listen as she began her story.

Recently while her boss, the HR Director, was on a river cruise in Vietnam with no internet access, a situation came up at work and, unfortunately, a perfect storm happened. The HR Manager, the second in command, had a medical emergency, went on leave, and was also not accessible. So, Bella was it, the only person in the HR office when the general manager's executive assistant called to summon her to the GM's office immediately.

"I was really nervous. I've only been at the hotel two months and only met the GM once, briefly, during my onboarding."

I nodded in understanding as she continued. "When I got up to his office, I was taken right in. The GM was behind his big desk, and the head of the food and beverage department was sitting across from him. Even though we'd met a couple of times when he came to HR, I never interacted with him. The executive assistant came back in with a coffee carafe and three cups and left closing the door behind her."

"Bella, that had to be so intimidating for you. How were you feeling?"

"I was shaking and didn't accept coffee or any other beverage because I couldn't have held anything in my hand. They knew I was nervous and tried to calm me down with small talk—how was my job going, did I enjoy working at the hotel. I answered yes, my job was very interesting, and the staff had warmly welcomed me to the team. Then the GM said, 'We've got a messy situation and I know this is a lot to ask of a new person, but you're going to have to handle it for us.'"

Bella said the food and beverage director seemed a little sheepish when the GM asked if she was aware of the practice that the banquet staff could drink left over alcohol while they cleaned up after the guests left. Since the GM didn't seem upset by hearing this, she assumed it must be an accepted practice. Then the bombshell dropped.

"After an event a few weeks ago, two employees who'd been drinking and flirting, started texting each other pictures—well, I guess they were sexting each other—and kept it up after the event. The woman claimed she tried to call a halt to it, but the man apparently wouldn't stop. She finally went to her manager and reported the incidents, said she wanted his texts and emails to stop, and asked if this was sexual harassment. When the manager called the man to his office to tell him to stop, the texter got really angry. He said it was consensual and had proof—a picture she'd sent him of her bare breasts, and you could see her face as well. He texted a copy of the picture to his manager."

I sat forward in my chair thinking this was a significant issue for a recent college grad to encounter, but I didn't want to deflate her confidence. Instead, I said, "You're right, this isn't a story you could have shared with the audience tonight. While it would have been interesting to hear ideas on how to handle it, I might have had trouble keeping control of the room. What happened next?" My thought was to give her a little breathing room, but she seemed anxious to get the story out and jumped right back to it.

"The manager brought the situation to the food and beverage director that morning along with the picture of the woman's breasts, and that's how I ended up involved. The GM told me to talk with the district HR director for guidance on next steps. They gave me the photo and asked me to report back, immediately, if not sooner. They both stood, shook my hand, and thanked me for my professionalism. You can only imagine how my knees were shaking as I took the elevator back to the HR offices. Did I mention, I hardly knew the district HR guy?"

When she got back to her office and calmed herself, Bella said she called the district HR director, told him what she knew, and asked for his help. He told her to get the woman in as quickly as possible, show her the photo she'd sent the man, and get her side of the story. Since banquet employees don't always work full time, she asked him what to do if the woman was not on the schedule until the coming weekend—four days away. He said, "Get it cleared with the GM to bring her in today if possible. He needs this resolved and quickly. Tell him I said to pay her for her time."

While I agreed with the strategy, I couldn't help but feel for Bella—having to go back to the GM. This district HR guy, as Bella called him, could have intervened. But Bella called the GM and got his permission to bring the employee in quickly, then called the woman and asked her to come in that afternoon, on her day off. The woman agreed to do so, likely thinking it was about her harassment claim. She certainly wasn't aware Bella had a revealing photo and had heard the other side of the story, albeit second hand.

"Oh dear," I said, "bet she was surprised when you filled her in with what you knew and that you had the photo she'd sent."

"Yes, but I'm not done with the bombshells yet. I told her we had the photo showing not only her face and breasts, but also her phone number, indicating she had consented to this relationship. Her face turned red, and she looked like she was going to start crying. Instead, she bent down, pulled a folder from her purse, and said she also had a picture—one he'd sent her. She opened the folder and handed me a picture of, well, a very private part of a male anatomy. It didn't have his face in it but showed it was sent from his phone. This whole thing apparently started as a harmless flirtation after a lot of whisky, but she wasn't interested in the flirtation going any farther. It was pretty unbelievable."

After the woman left, Bella called Sam, the district HR director, to fill him in on what she learned. He told her to bring the man in the following day for a meeting. He'd be there as a witness, but she would have to handle the meeting.

I could feel myself reacting to idea of a seasoned HR professional shirking his duty but didn't want Bella to see my annoyance. "It seems that Sam is a wimp—I can't imagine letting a new HR professional handle such a difficult situation, but I hope it means he had a lot of confidence in you—not that he didn't want to deal with it himself."

She rolled her eyes and sighed, "Well, I know I keep saying it gets worse, but it's the truth. I'd only met Sam once when he came to see my boss, and he pretty much ignored me then. The next day when he arrived for the meeting, he wasted no time telling me he didn't want to see the picture of the man's *privates*. He instructed me to show the picture to the man in a way where he, Sam, couldn't see it and to ask the guy to confirm it was indeed him."

"Is that what happened?"

"Yup. The guy came in all charged up thinking he was the one who had the upper hand because he'd turned the picture of her into his manager, but he sure had no idea we had *this* photo of him. So, I very calmly picked up the folder and held it so only he could see the picture and asked in as sweet a voice as I could muster at that moment, 'Is this your penis?'"

By now I was barely holding it together as I imagined this very young and new HR professional woman having to do this while a considerably older man with extensive HR experience sat quietly by. If he'd been in the room right now, I would have had a few choice words for him about his lack of professionalism and backbone—not to mention his management style. What kind of message was he sending to her?

The man admitted it was his penis, but argued it was all in fun. In fact, he claimed that the woman had posed for several pictures showing her breasts that a co-worker had taken during their shift, and pulled those pictures up on his phone, pointing out that you could see they were taken in the women's changing room. It also seemed that the woman had now turned her attention to some other guy and was sending him pictures of her breasts. Then he produced one of those pictures that the other guy had forwarded to him. It was clear that this picture, too, had been taken at work.

"Sam, who finally found his voice, told the guy he was to clean out his locker and leave the premises immediately. He would get his final check in the mail. Naturally, the guy couldn't leave it alone—he had to ask what was going to happen to the woman. I pulled myself together and told him it wasn't his concern and walked him to the door. Sam told me to call the woman involved in this situation and terminate her employment. Even though the man had sent the photo after she'd withdrawn consent, her behavior was unprofessional."

I assured Bella this was by far one of the strangest stories I'd ever heard in my HR career but also let her know if she stayed in HR, she probably would continue to be amazed at the things people do at work. She said she was going to have a long talk with her manager when she returned from vacation and then decide if the hotel was the place for her. I told her she had great instincts and hoped she'd stick with HR. There is so much more to HR's role in organizations than dealing with bad behavior at work, and she could add value in other facets of the profession. Now I knew why she'd taken off her nametag. I have to admit, I was curious which hotel she worked at, and as the speaker, I had access to the attendee list. It would be tempting to find out, but I decided it really didn't matter.

We walked together to the parking lot and found we were parked next to each other. She hugged me and thanked me for listening. I gave her my card and said I'd be available anytime if she needed advice or a sounding board.

* * *

The next day, Kyle Greene and I were flying to the St. Louis office for a meeting with all the regional HR team members. Driving from the airport to the office I gave him a summary of the story Bella had told me. I was really interested in hearing a man's perspective on this one.

He brushed his hair off his face as he listened, and I noticed he didn't ask his usual number of questions. One of the things I like best about Kyle is his curiosity but, in this case, he didn't seem to want to know more than I was telling him. In fact, he seemed a bit uncomfortable. Maybe he was embarrassed discussing something so personal with his female manager—he is a southern gentleman, after all—or maybe it's a *guy thing*. I made a mental note to ask my husband when I got home at the end of the week.

* * *

What a rare treat—a Saturday morning alone with my husband, Jack. Our twin daughters, Erin and Emily were at a sleepover, so Jack and I were enjoying a leisurely, uninterrupted breakfast. I used this opportunity to tell Jack, who's an employment attorney, the story Bella had shared with me. He seemed both horrified and amused. I imagine it was the labor attorney who was horrified, but the man with a wonderful sense of humor was amused.

"Jack, I told his story to Kyle on our trip and it seemed to make him a bit uncomfortable. Is that a *guy thing*?"

His eyes sparkled as he said, "Yes, I'd say most men are a bit uncomfortable when talking about a penis—especially at work with a woman no less—even if it isn't theirs."

I couldn't help but wonder if this was why Sam acted the way he did with Bella. Nevertheless, he needed to man up. Even if he was uncomfortable, didn't he realize how uncomfortable she was?

"Do you remember," Jack was saying, "the time I told you about my client who owns the chain of hair salons who had the problem with men *pleasuring themselves* under the cape or whatever it's called that they put over you when they're cutting or washing your hair? Imagine the surprise when a new stylist unsnapped the cape and pulled it off to find the guy unzipped and holding his penis. The client wanted to get a restraining order to keep the guy out of their shop, but I told them it wouldn't do much good in this situation. Besides, the guy would just go someplace else and do it. The amazing thing to me was when the client told me she'd asked around to her colleagues in the salon world and found almost every one of them had experienced something similar. It's so common that most salon owners let new stylists know it might happen, so they don't freak when it does."

I was laughing so hard the tears were streaming down my face when the door opened and our teenage daughters came in asking, "Mom, what's so funny?"

Jack and I looked at each other before he said, "Adult stuff—can't share."

The twins who are used to this answer from their parents, rolled their eyes, and went upstairs. I turned to Jack and said, "What's wrong with people or maybe I should say men? Other than you, is every man a latent pervert?"

Jack gave me a playful nudge. "You may be on to something. I had another client a long time ago who wanted me to come in and meet with the men in their organization about proper etiquette at the urinal.

Apparently, there were complaints from male staff about one of the guys who liked to peek at other men's *equipment* while standing too close at the urinal. Then there was the issue of someone, and it may have been at the same company, but I can't remember—there was a guy who they were pretty sure was jerking off in the men's room."

He said the client too small to have an HR department, so he served as a resource for issues like these, but drew the line at doing men's room etiquette training.

"And, I would have had the same reaction—HR has to handle a lot of messy situations, but I can't imagine doing a lunch and learn session for the men at Kings on that topic. What people do need is training or coaching on how to confront bad behavior in general."

"Good point," said Jack. "In fact, it's brilliant."

"I know. Isn't that why you married me? Changing the subject, don't know if I ever told you about by best friend in high school who worked in a chain retail store at our local mall. She called me one day after she left work and was laughing so hard, I thought she was crying. Apparently, a man came right up to her with an arm full of dresses and asked her if she'd model them for her. He said he had a daughter about her age and wanted to buy her something but needed to see it on a person. She did as he asked and each time, he'd ask her to twirl. She noticed he was standing behind a high stack of sweaters on a table and all she could see was his face but later, after he'd left, the other sales associates laughingly told her that he'd done this before, and they referred to him as Mr. Ever-hard."

This time, it was Jack who was crying with laughter. "I know you'd led quite a sheltered life, Honey, but did you even understand what they were implying?"

"Sort of—I mean I wasn't totally naïve but it sure was a learning experience. And, I was about the same age as our daughters are now. Maybe we shouldn't let them leave the house."

As we moved through our day of usual family Saturday stuff, my mind kept wandering to what we'd been sharing that morning. Both Jack and I deal with people issues all the time in our jobs—and you can never predict what people will do. Boredom is not a word you hear in our world and as I say at least several times a day—what's wrong with people?

CHAPTER 5

We've Come a Long Way

The relationships formed in our networking group have moved beyond collegial bonds that focus on business issues. Strong personal relationships have formed as well. We reach out to each other when we need help with personal issues too.

As he pulled into the Chicago Marina, David Morgan spotted Jason Edison and his sailboat right away. Jason had taken his boat out of the water for the upcoming winter season, and David had agreed to help him secure it in dry dock in exchange for an early dinner at a popular downtown Chicago sports bar where they could watch the Bears' game after they finished their work.

"Great timing," Jason said, a big grin on his face. "I just got here just a few minutes ago myself. Ready to get to work?"

"Aye aye, captain!" David said. Then noticing the grin on Jason's face, "What's so amusing?"

"Nothing, really," Jason replied. "It's just so refreshing to see a colleague out of his normal business environment, relaxed, and in jeans."

"It's all about the balance we strive for," said David. "But I do want to bend your ear over something semi-business related."

"Can't give it a rest, can you, David?" Jason said motioning for him to follow him over to the sailboat, with a ladder already leaning against it. Starting up the ladder, Jason turned to David, "Welcome aboard, mate. You can tell me what's on your mind as we work."

In his haste to board the boat, David almost missed a step on the ladder. "Did you happen to read the article in this morning's Chicago Tribune about more health care providers agreeing to cover gender reassignment surgery?"

"I did," responded Jason. "And while it will have no immediate impact on my company, I was struck by the seismic shift in policy and social issues this represents. Remember when the medical community changed its professional consensus about gender dysphoria and stopped calling it gender identity disorder to remove any associated stigma? Not too different from how the human resources profession evolves."

Squinting as the sun reflected off something shiny on the deck, he paused. "Why the interest, David? Are you wrestling with a related issue at work?"

David explained he was giving a guest lecture to a group of graduate students at University of Chicago next month, and he thought this would be a great example to use about changing social mores and their impact on business. It also caused him to recall a situation he'd encountered early in his career. He wanted to stress the importance of data, but also bring the human side into it. While only a small percent of Americans identified as transgender, the number seemed to be growing and yet, there's been resistance to provide benefits to them for so long. Without insurance, the out-of-pocket costs for hormone therapy and surgeries can vary greatly and be prohibitive. "This generation is so much more accepting of differences. I'd like to get input from colleagues who've been in HR longer to illustrate how issues and policies evolve," he said.

Jason motioned to the ropes laying on the deck. "Can you pick up those dock lines and put them into that box, please?" As he started tossing cushions into the cabin below, he said, "Tell me more about your past experience while we work. We can finish talking about it later, over dinner and some beers."

David explained this occurred when he was a recruiter, although his duties were expanding. A new manager had come into his office, perplexed about an employee in his department named Adam. The manager assumed Adam was a male but had started overhearing comments that suggested otherwise. The predominantly female department members were snidely referring to Adam as Eve. The manager was trying to be sensitive to the employee's situation and gather information. David, unfortunately, had little to contribute, but they both agreed to keep eyes and ears open. Suddenly, Adam started showing up to work in dresses and the situation escalated beyond snide comments. David's manager, the Director of HR, got involved. Everyone was complaining how uncomfortable they were around *shim*. While appearing flamboyant at work, Adam was reluctant to share any details about his personal situation, leaving everyone at the time wondering if he was a cross dresser, transgender, or was it something else? Someone even commented if he was going to dress like a woman, he'd better learn to sit like a lady and keep his legs together when he wore a skirt. David remembered that the company and Adam agreed it was best if Adam resigned.

"How differently this situation would be handled today," David said.

"It would," agreed Jason looking at his watch. "Let's put these tools away and clean up. Plenty of time to get to O'Toole's before the game starts."

When they arrived, David slid into the first open booth they saw as Jason stopped at the bar to get a pitcher of beer. As he joined David, the waitress, wearing a Bears jersey, was right behind him with two menus. They quickly placed their order. "Good choices—Streeterville angus beef burger, medium rare, with sweet potato fries, and shepherd's pie," she said flashing them a smile. "Hope the Bears' defense comes to play today. Last week was a disaster."

As Jason reached for the mugs to pour the beer, David laid out his plan for his lecture next month, asking Jason if he thought it was a viable subject and a good approach. Jason leaned back in the booth, stretching his arms overhead and working the soreness out of his muscles from the morning's work.

"I do think it's a good approach, David. You've seen attitudes change on many issues, and I've seen a lot more. Folks entering business and HR, especially the younger ones, have to understand gender reassignment and transgender issues weren't always accepted. Then again, neither was sexual orientation. I've spoken with younger colleagues who don't understand the fuss. They have a great appreciation of differences and feel strongly that differences should be accepted. Yet, they often don't understand that the leaders in their organizations—the very people they have to persuade to make changes involving money—often come from a time when differences weren't understood nor accepted. Sharing stories and experiences is great. It gives the personal and historical perspective—so often lost today. If these are grad students, they already know that presenting a business case for change involves analytics and hard data. Your idea of presenting anecdotal evidence too strikes a balance. It makes the point the business case involves both human and financial issues. They've got to be prepared to address both. The evolution theme is good too, especially the evolution within the medical profession. It makes a powerful message and shows history."

David was sitting back, sipping his beer. Jason was providing a good reality check for his idea. "That leads me to my next question. Do you have any stories about this issue you can share?"

"I do," said Jason, checking his watch, just as the waitress returned with their meals.

"Enjoy, gentlemen."

Jason picked up his folk and tasted his shepherd's pie. David could tell he was forming his thoughts as deliberately as he was eating his food. Finally, he said, "I had one situation that worked out very well. One of the reasons it did—I learned a lesson from another colleague whose situation didn't turn out quite so well. Let's start with the ill-fated one."

"It seems there was this highly valued employee in the tech department. He was married and had two children. He was well regarded by his colleagues and management. Suddenly, people started noticing subtle changes. First it was foundation makeup, then eyeliner. His manicured nails were going from clear polish, to light color, and finally to brightly colored acrylic nails like many of the women wore. Then he was spotted one weekend outside of work wearing women's clothing. The employee who spotted him came to HR apparently concerned he was in crisis."

David was quietly listening. "Then what?"

Jason explained the employee finally announced he was going through the transition to become a woman. It was going to be a lengthy process, partially because there was no insurance coverage. In addition to the hormone therapy, there were going to be multiple operations including Adam's apple removal and a genital change, an operation only a small percentage of transwomen have. Throughout the change, he dressed as a woman making colleagues uncomfortable. The segregated restrooms created more anxiety. The company wanted to accommodate him by building a unisex restroom, but the building management and owners were opposed. The lawyers had to get involved to make it happen. Once his surgeries were finally completed, he legally changed from a man to a woman, but the employees couldn't accept her. Her name changed from Warren to Wendy, but people kept calling her Warren. Her marriage ended, but she still had financial responsibility for the children. She finally left the company thinking it would be better somewhere else. She found a job outside of the IT field.

"Did anyone ever hear from or about her again?" asked David.

"Gina, my colleague, ran into her at a job fair about two years later. Wendy was looking to get back into IT but having a hard time. Gina felt terrible when she slipped and called her Warren. She sensed Wendy was struggling financially and wished the company had done more to help with Wendy's medical bills."

When did this happened? Do you know?"

"Early to mid-90s, I think, why?" said Jason.

"The situation I told you about earlier today occurred around the same time. What's interesting is I don't think my company at the time ever found out—or cared to know—if Adam was planning gender reassignment. And he certainly wasn't willing to talk about it."

"Different companies, different cultures. People weren't comfortable with the issue then," said Jason. Looking up at the TV, he realized the pregame show was almost over and kick-off would be in about five minutes. Since the game was about to begin, the guys turned their attention to the TV screens around the pub.

By half-time, everyone was exuberant—the Bears had just scored a touchdown. The waitress returned offering another pitcher of beer. David hesitated, then said, "Better not." So, Jason ordered an apple cobbler to split and two cups of coffee, feeling guilty they were taking up her booth and not drinking any more beer.

"Time for the other story," said Jason. "An issue at my last company, several years after Gina's experience. This time, it was a woman transitioning to a man. When she came to me initially, it was to discuss benefits. We didn't have the coverage for gender reassignment surgery at the time but were investigating it. Then she told me she'd be starting hormone therapy soon and presenting as a man. She was anxious about how it would be accepted at work. I took the issue to my CEO—a great guy—very committed to putting the company at the forefront of helping our employees."

With top management support and involvement from the employee, Jason was able to formulate a plan. The employee suggested an outside expert who dealt with these issues. Recognizing there'd be a lot of discomfort, even animosity, they met with the expert and planned a series of employee meetings to explain to the coworkers what was happening. The expert was able to field questions like, "When you take the hormones, will you be angry?" which showed how little they understood. The company's goal was to have the employee treated with dignity and respect. A unisex bathroom was built near his work area. Announcements were made and the employee had input into all of the communications—the ones advising employees about the meetings with the experts and the ones about the unisex bathroom. The company even set up an employee council to deal with this and related issues.

"Seems like a lot of effort and resources for one employee," David said.

"Remember," replied Jason. "not just the transgender employee was affected. Everyone in the workplace was—coworkers and managers. They're all part of the human side. The leadership team saw the wisdom in making the investment, especially in the outside expert and employee council. For one thing, if people were sitting around gossiping, they weren't being productive. It wasn't all altruistic. There were business drivers as well."

"But, what about the employee? Did he appreciate the efforts?" David asked.

"He did. He appreciated the involvement. Frustrated at times because he was still being referred to as *she*, I had to remind him that people had known him as a woman for many years. It was going to take time. It was a process—another example of evolution."

"The level of support from leadership. Were you surprised by it, Jason?"

"At first, yes, but I learned the source behind the CEO's support—the other reason this situation was successful. In the mid-1980s my CEO was working for a company in California, no less. An employee had confided to several co-workers he was being tested for AIDS. When the employee didn't return that afternoon or the next day, people started speculating and freaking out. Remember, it was the 1980s. At that time, people thought casual contact could transmit the HIV virus. Not only was information about AIDS just emerging, but more misinformation was being shared than facts. And even though this was near Los Angeles where the gay community was less closeted at the time, there was still a lot of bias against them."

Jason noticed the corners of David's mouth curl up in a smile. "What?"

"Just think if they'd had the Internet and social media back then. Anyway, what happened next?"

"After three days he was a no show and they considered it job abandonment. But it didn't quell people's fears. The company contacted the Human Rights Commission and brought in a doctor to talk with the employees in his department. It became very contentious. The employee got wind of it and threatened to sue, even though the company had no information confirming his medical condition nor mentioned his name in the meeting with the doctor. Given this experience, my CEO was adamant about transparency. He wanted the transgender employee involved in all aspects. He remembered the climate when people didn't want to talk about AIDS. Or even sexual orientation, for that matter. AIDS was such a new issue in the 80s, not unlike transgender-related issues are today. He saw similarities and wanted to handle this differently. He didn't want to relive anything remotely close to that experience again."

"Jason, this makes me think of something I should try to work into my presentation. People often assume that all companies are heartless—run by unfeeling robots chasing the bottom line. In fact, they're run by people—people who bring their own experiences and yes, human compassion, to work every day. Those experiences and compassion influence the decisions that leaders make."

Jason looked up at the TV screen. Yes, he'd have time to finish the discussion before the third quarter began.

"Looking back, anything you'd do differently?"

Jason raised his folded hands up to his chin. "One thing. I suggested the guys invite him out for drinks, poker, something like that. It didn't go over well at all. I realized I was trying too hard to change people's beliefs and attitudes. All we could do was to make sure he was treated respectfully at work."

"One last question," David said quickly, realizing the third quarter was about to begin. "Did he stay with the company?"

"That was a close one," Jason sighed. "He almost left because the insurance didn't cover his medical expenses. We'd already gotten approval to add it, but it wouldn't take effect for a few months. He was anxious to move forward, but then realized all the company had done for him. If he went someplace else just for insurance, he might lose all the support and understanding he'd gained from his colleagues. He decided it was worth the wait."

The waitress returned with the cobbler—divided onto two plates—and coffee. Jason began tasting it slowly, thinking back on the events leading to his company offering the needed medical benefits. The biggest push back came from the insurance carrier, who was arguing against it, but the leadership team, including the CFO, was on board—even knowing there was an employee in the wings waiting take advantage of the benefit as soon as it was implemented. He looked up at David thinking *I'm about seven years older than David and have struggled with some difficult issues, issues that weren't as difficult for him. And our younger generation of peers don't see why these issues are difficult. How we've evolved.*

Taking a sip of his coffee, he continued. "The insurance company was resisting our decision and we were getting very frustrated with them. We were self-insured—assuming the financial risk for health care benefits. We suspected they didn't want to start a precedent. Hell, I can remember when preventative care wasn't covered. When we got pap smears and mammograms included—after a battle—my benefits director happily declared I was a feminist. I guess I am."

"Y'know, Jason, attitudes toward gender identity, sexual orientation and sex discrimination have been emerging on so many fronts. I attended a conference a few years ago where cases were discussed involving federal employees before the Equal Employment Opportunity Commission. In one case it was determined that discrimination against a transgender individual because she's transgender is sex discrimination. Another said that discrimination because of sexual orientation is discrimination on the basis of sex. Both violated Title VII of the Civil Rights Act. At the time I thought this something to keep an eye on. Look at where we are now. The Supreme Court has agreed—another example of social evolution."

Jason was watching the ice cream melt on his piece of cobbler. "When we were growing up in HR, if you will, the spectrum of issues around sexual orientation and gender identity weren't on the radar screen in any corporate setting. Now, it's not a matter of accepting differences— it's embracing them. For these up-and-coming professionals, differences are no big deal. This discussion we've been having is a good example of how in times past, sexual orientation and gender identity were foreign concepts and kept tucked in the shadows. Change didn't happen that fast and people held strongly to traditional social views. Today, social change, like changing technology, is happening at lightning speed. The younger generations are used to that pace. Their world is fluid, and culturally interconnected. Gender identity is frequently in the news—bathroom bills or expansion of LGBTQ rights—indications of changing social values. In the past, it took more time for attitudes to catch up with these types of changes."

"Agreed. More proof that we can't take our eyes off the horizon. Issues such as these can change the landscape quickly. In the past, business often wanted to keep out of social issues. But as these issues evolve, they can't be ignored by business leaders. And many want to be more socially responsible."

By the end of the third quarter, the Bears were clearly losing—21-7. David stretched, realizing it had been quite a long day already. "I think I'll head out. I've got a longer drive home than you do."

With that, Jason yawned. "I think I'll join you. Let me settle the tab, and I'll walk out with you."

Driving home, with the game on the radio, David found himself thinking about Adam whom that new manager had inquired about so long ago. Adam likely wasn't a cross-dresser, but rather a transgender individual going through the transition. No wonder the process took so long in the past. People couldn't afford it. As he recalled, Adam was not highly paid. Another important lesson that he wanted to be sure to incorporate—behind all these policy issues—public or private policy issues—there are people whose lives are affected—real people, with real situations and real lives. That's why these issues need attention, and that's why they constantly evolve. Many people don't think we've come far enough, but you've got to understand where we've been to measure our progress. He couldn't help wondering about the challenges the students he'd be addressing are facing now—like non-binary individuals who don't identify as either male or female—and the challenges they'll face in the future.

CHAPTER 6

Affairs, Lies & ...

I was running late which is not unusual for me. I spied Allison in a booth near the back of the Fontera Grill—Rick Bayless' famous restaurant on Clark Street. We've been trying to get a reservation here for months, so I was glad she had arrived on time to hold the table. Allison Walters is a young HR professional whom I am informally mentoring. I noticed she was intently looking at the booth across from where she was sitting, so I glanced over and saw a couple sitting so close together you couldn't see where he started or she ended. The way they were gazing into each other's eyes made you feel the sparks. I made my way past them and Allison jumped up and enveloped me in a warm hug.

Allison is one of the smartest young people I know. She hasn't been out of college long but seems more mature than other people her age. We have wonderful discussions about people, work, and life in general. I enjoy spending time with her. Not only does she seek my advice, but she challenges me as well. She has so many unique perspectives and is never at a loss for words. I've always thought the reason she speaks quickly is that she has a lot to say and wants to be heard. And she always shares interesting stories about her dating life—some of which make me anxious as I think of what's ahead for my teenage daughters. Hopefully, all that I learn from Allison will help me navigate what's coming with the twins.

Not only is Allison smart, she is kind and considerate, and funny, but she always puts others first. That is such a great quality for anyone in business, so I have no doubts she is going to be a great success in whatever challenge she takes on.

"Allison, it's so good to see you. Why does it take so long for us to find time to talk?" I am a firm believer in the value of mentors. I've had many wonderful people whom I learned from over my career. Allison and I try to get together once a month, but it can be difficult as she is working for a management consulting practice and travels a lot—both for business and for pleasure. I love getting together to hear where she has been and what she's seen or observed with clients or others. Allison is one of those people who never stops learning and growing professionally. We met when I spoke at an HR conference, and she approached me afterwards to ask some great questions. Since then, she's completed her MBA and who knows what will be next.

The server handed me a menu. We each ordered a glass of red wine and told her we'd need some time before we ordered dinner. She flashed us a smile as she told us to just signal her when we were ready, and she'd come right back.

Allison turned toward me. "Maryanne, you look fantastic. What have you done with your hair? I love it"

"I finally let Henri talk me into going shorter, and it is taking some getting used to. Glad you like it."

"I do and no way do you look like the mother of 16-year-old daughters."

"Why thank you," I laughed delighted the wine had arrived. We toasted to good health and both sipped our wine.

"Let's order quickly so I can tell you my latest challenges from my crazy clients," Allison said. We quickly looked at the menu then closed them to indicate we were ready to order. As she had promised, our server came right over and took our orders.

As the server walked away, Allison began talking in her staccato style. "I may have told you we have several clients in Springfield that are federal government contractors. So, I was down there last month for a series of meetings with a major contractor and got pulled into a messy situation." She paused as the server brought her salad and my soup.

I tried to eat my soup but quickly realized it was too hot. I put down my spoon and turned my attention to Allison who had already started talking. "I'd taken the train down from Chicago and walked over to the client's offices. I'd barely taken off my coat when the client's executive assistant told me that Tamika, the HR Generalist, needed to see me immediately. Since the executive assistant sets up my schedule on my monthly visits, she knew my day was totally booked. We took a quick look at the schedule before I asked her to move a couple of meetings and cancel my lunch so I could get right to whatever Tamika's issue was. This was highly unusual, but I guess it's what we deal with in our world."

Allison stopped talking long enough to take a sip of wine and start on her salad. My soup had cooled down enough for me to eat while she continued talking.

"I went to Tamika's office and she appeared very happy to see me—she'd even hugged me which she never did before that day. We sat down and she jumped right into the issue—it was clear she was dying to talk about it."

"Tamika said that last week one of their senior vice presidents, a retired general, asked his administrative assistant to make a copy of his desktop's hard drive that afternoon while he attended a meeting. He'd asked her to copy files before but never a hard drive, so she asked him why he hadn't put in a request for IT to do it. Apparently, he didn't want to involve IT especially since they were moving to cloud-based computing. But he asked if she would keep this just between them. She said she thought this request was out of line, but he was her boss so she didn't want to make him angry—he has the reputation of being easily upset and loves to fire people. She went to Tamika and asked if she could be in any trouble if she copied the drive. Tamika said she'd get back to her about whether IT should get involved but, in the meantime, not to do anything. She was pretty sure that the general's computer might contain company sensitive or confidential info that wasn't supposed to be copied."

As I finished my soup and took a sip of wine, I smiled at Allison. "Isn't it amazing the things HR has to handle on a daily basis?"

"You're not going to believe what happened next," she said. "Tamika talked with their IT director who said this was a highly unusual request but because it was the general who'd asked, they'd do it. He had one of his technicians copy the drive and, you'll never guess what they found."

"Company confidential information," I laughed while signaling her to keep talking.

"Yes, but if only that was all," Allison said. "There was a long string of emails that clearly showed he and Felicia, another senior vice president, were having an affair. Emails with attachments—like photos of the two of them having sex on his office couch. There were texts of his genitals that he'd sent to her with invitations to come right to his office because he was *ready and waiting*." She put down her fork and stared out into the restaurant. "Do you believe people?"

"No, I don't," I said. "And you must have been pretty shocked to hear this. Allison, is this client on a government facility and is this a government computer? If so, aren't there rules about misuse of government equipment?"

"No, it's the client's site, but they do have rules about using the company's computers and stuff like that, which they take seriously and do enforce."

"What did you do?"

"I asked if they'd confronted the general and Felicia yet and Tamika said yes, both of them had been put on administrative leave and escorted out of the building by security. They also seized Felicia's computer hard drive which revealed even more damaging photos of them having sex in her office too. There were emails outlining times they'd met in hotels when they were traveling on government business. Since they were both married to other people, there were a lot of messages about how difficult it was to find time to be together."

"When did this lust affair start?" I asked, knowing Allison loved a good play on words.

"Apparently, they'd first hooked up at a conference they'd attended in Washington, DC and went on from there. They'd fallen in love—at least she said she loved him and shared her plans to divorce her husband if he would leave his wife. From the emails, it didn't sound like he was inclined to mess up his life by getting a divorce. He'd had quite a distinguished career in the military, and there were rumors his wife had family money which he knew he'd lose in a divorce."

Allison got a strange look on her face and said, "Tamika was really freaked by something else they found in the general's office—a jar of what was later found to be urine in one of his desk drawers. What's that about?"

"Allison, I wish I could tell you that's the most bizarre thing I've ever heard, but it's not. And you're likely to hear many more weird things throughout your career, too."

"Anyway, the search of his office also uncovered his company laptop was missing so IT went to his house to pick it up. The general was highly confrontational and threatened legal action but finally let them take the laptop."

Allison let out a long sigh. "None of this makes sense. He knew what was on his hard drive so why did he want it copied. He should have been researching how to totally scrub it and then, there's his laptop which he had at his house. It also contained gross pictures of him and Felicia having sex, emails they exchanged and company confidential info. His wife certainly could have opened it at any time and found the evidence of his affair."

Our entrees had arrived so we each started to eat. "So if I have this straight, Allison, he had compromising pictures and personal emails on his company's desktop, he wanted its entire hard drive copied—pictures, emails *and* company confidential info—which he likely intended to remove from the premises—and he placed that confidential info on his laptop which he did remove from work—all in violation of the policy."

"Oh," said Allison, "did I mention that in addition to the sex pictures of them there was a video? So, there's actually proof of them doing it right in his office. GRRoss!"

"Well it seems like there were several policy violations, not the least of which was the general's removing company confidential information from the site which I'm sure is grounds for immediate termination. So, you walked into this situation after the general and Felicia were on administrative leave, but I'm guessing they wanted your help on the termination details."

"Right you are." Allison said finishing a bite of her dinner. "Tamika shared she'd already received a call from an attorney representing the general and Felicia requesting they be allowed to resign so they could keep their government clearances."

"They didn't think about that when they fell into lust, did they?" I laughed.

"No, they didn't. Tamika asked for my advice on what I thought they should do. Then, she added yet another bombshell—the general and Felicia were scheduled to make a presentation at an industry conference coming up soon. What to do about that? The organization didn't want any of this to leak out since the general and Felicia were both so highly visible in the government, but they didn't want any proprietary information being shared either."

"So how did things end up, Allison?"

"When I left that Friday, the decision was made to allow them to resign and have them sign a release to not take any action against the company. Security did advise their attorney that reports were required to be made about their conduct to the appropriate agency that oversees their clearances and no guarantees could be made. The government agency and not the company makes those decisions regarding clearances. They were also told if they used any company information at the upcoming conference or ever, they would be sued. I heard from Tamika today—the general and Felicia *did* go to the conference but did not present. Another of the executives was there and said they were behaving like nothing was wrong but kept their distance from him. I'll ask again—do you believe people?"

I smiled to let her know I understood where she was coming from. "I know this kind of behavior at work seems amazing to you at this point in your career and your life. Your parents have been happily married for 30 years and I remember your grandparents celebrated their 60th anniversary last year. However, there are lots of people who aren't as true to their marriage vows as they should be." I caught myself before saying more so as not to sound so judgmental. I really worked hard not to interject my personal beliefs onto others but sometimes, it was impossible not to.

"Allison, I remember when I first heard about infidelity at work. I was in high school and worked after school and on weekends at a small grocery chain in our neighborhood. I was at the checkout station one busy Saturday when a woman came in the front door with a gun, shouting at the top of her lungs, 'Where's Tessa—I know she's here someplace. I want to see her now.' Tessa was our assistant manager. I slumped down below my register so I couldn't be seen, but I could see that the woman with the gun spotted Tessa and rushed toward her. I saw customers running from the building, and I was terrified. Then the woman screamed she knew Tessa was having an affair with her son-in-law, the store manager."

Allison looked horrified and said, "Maryanne, how awful. How old were you?"

"I'd just turned 17. I remember because I loved Seventeen Magazine and turning 17 was a really big deal—I thought I was so grown up."

Wide-eyed, Allison leaned in and whispered, "Was there shooting or what happened next?"

I told her the police took the woman away and we all tried to go back to work. My mother found out later that most of the staff knew about the affair, but I was young and naïve and didn't have a clue. This incident brought out a real problem in that company. Turns out the district manager was taking kickbacks from suppliers, and the manager knew about it. In exchange for keeping quiet, the district manager overlooked the affair. Looking back, I can't help but pity the poor HR person who had to deal with that mess.

Allison frowned as I finished my story. "Honestly, I know I am pretty new to the working world, but I had no idea people having affairs at work is so prevalent."

"Think about it," I replied. "Most of us spend much more time at work than we do at home, so I guess it's bound to happen. But it would be nice if people could just be friends and not lovers—especially if they're already married to other individuals—since their actions impact so many other people, including their families and their organizations. I sure have seen it happen everywhere I work—even at Kings Family Restaurants. Some of our restaurants are open 24 hours which creates interesting opportunities for affairs, I guess. I got a call one day from the wife of one of our restaurant managers—let's call him Leo. She said she was sure he was having an affair and named the woman she said was the other party. Before we could confront them, the District Manager made a surprise visit to the restaurant and asked to see Leo. One of the employees said he'd find him in his office. He found the manager *and* a female assistant manager scrambling to put on their clothes. The investigation showed the employees all knew about what was going on but didn't say anything because they feared retaliation."

Allison laughed. "How embarrassing. Were they both fired?"

"Sometimes it seems so obvious that termination is the only answer and if it had been up to me, they both would have been gone, if for nothing else than being away from their jobs when they should have been overseeing the restaurant operations. But this restaurant was in an area where most of the neighborhood was from Korea and Leo spoke fluent Korean, so Ralph convinced me the best decision was to discipline them both but not fire them. Of course, we couldn't fire her and not him and risk a discrimination charge, so the assistant manager was transferred to another restaurant. But the story didn't end there. Leo really had a lot of potential—he probably would be a vice president now, but this affair damaged his career with Kings. He never went beyond store manager and left us a few years later. I have no idea what happened to his marriage."

Allison looked almost sad as I finished my story. "So, what you're telling me is organizations can't prevent people from hooking up at work so I should just get over it."

"Yes, you're partly right—it is going to happen no matter how many policies organizations put in place prohibiting employees from dating or whatever—which, by the way, never work. Organizations can only address business issues and not personal issues unless the personal issue impacts the organization, and this can be frustrating for HR in particular. But I don't think you have to *get over it* as you say. Your personal values are important, and I hope you keep them even if others don't behave quite the same way you might think they should."

I touched my fingertips together. "All this talk of affairs at work reminds me of some other stories—examples of how this issue can come to haunt you."

Allison pulled her chair closer. "Do tell…"

Just then the server came over and asked if we wanted dessert—we didn't—or coffee. I looked at Allison and asked, "How about a glass of wine at the bar before we head for the subway?" She agreed so I asked the server to bring the check.

Once we paid the check, we made our way to the bar settling into comfortable chairs in the middle of the room. "So," said Allison, "you were saying…"

"Well, when I was working for the consulting firm after college, I was a very idealistic person at the time—never expected there'd be personal relationships in the office that would impact me. My small office was right across from Irene's, the office manager's very lush office. She had been with the firm for a long time and wielded a great deal of power. Usually her door was open, but one day it occurred to me one of the partners, Frank, spent a great deal of time in her office with the door closed. Then, I was assigned to work on a project with Frank and realized he knew far more than he should have about my personal life. He shared information with me which made me very uncomfortable, and I couldn't figure out how he knew it in the first place. When I shared my concern with a co-worker one evening at a happy hour, he laughed so hard his beer came out his nose—not a pretty sight. He told me Frank and Irene had been sleeping together for years, and she tells him everything she knows. He cautioned me to be very careful about what I said to her or who spent time in my office because she doesn't miss a thing and passes it all on to Frank."

Allison looked at me wide-eyed. "Couldn't you have done something?"

"I was horrified and couldn't believe this could be tolerated in a major management consulting firm, but my colleague reminded me of how much power the partners have, and I should just be smart and keep my office door closed. This issue never left me, and it's a good thing. Frank and Irene were in a consensual relationship. But that was no excuse for them gossiping about everyone else. Since I entered HR and started dealing with people, I've thought of Frank and Irene when I've counseled employees about being aware of how their actions may hurt others."

As we sipped our wine, Allison and I chatted about life outside of work. I told her Jack and I were taking the twins on a college hunting trip over the upcoming spring break. They have a long list of possibilities and are still trying to decide if they will go to the same school.

"I know I am going to miss them terribly when they go off to college in less than two years, but Jack is going to fall apart. He is such a sentimental guy."

Allison shared she'd met a new man recently and had a few dates. They'd met through friends and appeared to have similar interests. She said he was really cute and a good kisser, but it was too soon to tell if it would go anywhere. They were going to dinner and a movie this Friday night and she was hoping to get a better sense of whether he was interested in moving the relationship forward.

"Speaking of relationships, time for one more story? A colleague of mine worked in HR for a large company somewhere out west. She said one day two women came to see her complaining about a third woman in their department who was getting preferential treatment from their male boss and they suspected the two—who were both single—were dating. The company had a policy stipulating people in a relationship couldn't supervise the other person, so she called the two people into her office and asked if they were involved in a romantic relationship. They denied it. She said if they were, the company would transfer one of them to another department with no discipline involved. Again, they denied being together."

"And...?" Allison asked

"So, a few days later, the two women went to their VP and shared that the couple was now married but keeping it a secret. When confronted again, the couple continued denying any personal relationship. The VP investigated and discovered they'd been issued a marriage license. He told my HR friend to fire them both—not because they'd gotten married—but because they lied and tried to cover it up. But that is not the end of the story. The company terminated both of them and the fall out was fast and huge. The man involved was a favorite of other executives and well-liked by everyone. Several top executives came to my friend's office and actually screamed at her, saying *she* shouldn't have terminated him. Clearly, *she* didn't terminate them and was in fact against it. The termination was a company decision—the VP's decision—but people blamed her, and she took the brunt of their anger. She left soon thereafter and now works for a place where HR is valued."

After we finished our wine, we made our way to the subway where we took separate lines. I connected to the train to the suburbs and Allison had a short ride to her Near North apartment. On the way home I remembered my peer networking group was meeting soon. I so look forward to those meetings where we all feel so comfortable and are able to freely share our issues. One of the hardest parts about the HR world is we keep so many secrets, and there are so few people we can trust. Not only am I able to confidently share information with the group, they've become trusted advisors—and I'm pretty sure they feel the same way about me.

It was great to see Allison, and I'm glad I finally got to enjoy the wonderful food and service at Fontera Grill. Jack and I need to go there soon.

CHAPTER 7

What's Wrong with People?

There is always mass confusion at the beginning of each networking group meeting, especially if everyone enters the room at once. With greetings and hugs and getting settled, this month's will be no different, especially since we had a short break from our monthly meetings over the holidays, and everyone will be able to make it tonight.

I'd arrived before the others, and David Morgan couldn't believe I was the first one there. "You probably have the longest drive to get here, yet you beat everyone else."

"I know. I'm surprised too since I got caught on my way out of the office with yet another challenging situation," I said as we walked to the conference room near his office. "I can't wait to share with the group. I've missed our interesting discussions with people who understand the murky world of HR."

His phone buzzed and he looked down. "Maybe they all carpooled. The receptionist just texted there are four people in the lobby for me—be right back."

As I waited, I wandered around looking at the artwork and the office design—so reflective of the firm's culture. Since we're about to move into new space, insights from David would be helpful. I'm on the office move team, and I want to make sure the office design we pick is right for *our* culture.

A few minutes later, David came in with our colleagues. We took our seats laughing that at every meeting we each tended to sit in the same place. "Creatures of habit," said Jason Edison as he took his seat at the head of the table. I think he sits there so he can observe everyone.

It was so good to see Linda Goodman. She had missed our last meeting because she and her wife, Millie, had taken a cruise to celebrate their 25 years together by finally getting married. Linda left the corporate world a few years ago to join a successful executive search firm in Chicago and always has great stories and even better insights to add to our discussions. She has a unique way of showing the artistic side of her personality. Usually it was through the eye-catching accessories she wore to compliment her stylish outfits. Today it was a soft blue streak down the right side of her light-brown hair that accentuated her blue eyes. She said she had it done as a way to hang on to the memory of the cruise just a bit longer.

David, who was sitting next to Linda, turned to her and said, "I wish all I had to deal with when it comes to workplace appearance is whimsical, colored hair rather than some people's lack of propriety when it comes to what to wear to work." He smiled as he brushed a stray hair off the silk shirt he wore with the collar open—a new and relaxed look for him. David was having a bit of a problem adjusting to a less formal work environment at the tech company after years working at the very buttoned up culture of the Chicago School System.

Looking around the room I could tell everyone was dying to hear what would come next from David, and he didn't disappoint us.

"This morning one of the other VP's came to see me. I could tell he was uncomfortable, so we did the small talk routine for a while. After we'd covered the weather and Chicago sports, I finally asked Hal what was on his mind." The smile had left David's face.

To lighten the mood, I said, "Can we guess what came next?"

David leaned back in his chair. "In the interest of getting you all home before the next snowstorm hits, let me get to the point. Hal told me he was pretty sure his very young and very attractive female administrative assistant wasn't wearing underwear."

There were some suppressed giggles. We knew David wasn't joking, and this was seriously weighing on him. Jason turned, pointing his tented fingers toward his left. "David, was this guy serious—I mean it's work, not a club. And what did he mean she wasn't wearing underwear—no bra or what and even better—how did he know?"

I glanced around at the other women at the table and saw everyone looked a little sheepish. Linda was gazing down doodling in the small notebook she always carries, and Stephanie Packard was fidgeting with her reading glasses, probably contemplating the conversation she would have with this young woman. This kind of situation can't be easy for anyone to handle. While David could be fun loving among his peers, he was always cautious about inappropriate discussions in his workplace. To break the silence I said, "So, what did you say or do?"

David pushed his coffee to the middle of the table. "I asked Hal why he felt she wasn't wearing underwear, and he told me she had been working in his office getting old files ready for scanning and, well, he asked if I'd ever seen the movie Basic Instinct with Richard Gere and Sharon Stone—the scene when the sexy actress uncrossed her legs to reveal she wasn't wearing anything under her short skirt. I knew immediately where this was going and asked if this was the first time he'd been aware of this. He said he'd been suspicious a few times that she wasn't wearing a bra but really tried not to pay too close attention—sexual harassment and all— but this was different. Not wearing a bra is bad enough, but no panties?"

Stephanie put down her reading glasses and looked across the table at David. "Then what? Have you spoken to her yet?"

"Not yet, Stephanie. We're working through the best approach. Hal's concerned she may claim sexual harassment if he talks to her, and I told him he definitely can't talk to her alone about it."

"Isn't there a female staff member who could step in and have the conversation?"

"Can I enlist you for a few days, Steph? She'd warm right up to you. But yes, there is a female director on Hal's staff I think we can quietly ask who could have the conversation without it being obvious."

Jason got up and brought the plate of cookies to the table. "I never had to deal with this issue taking place in the office but did have to counsel a woman who came to our holiday party in a very tight, short, low cut white dress and proceeded to dance provocatively. It didn't take long for the guys, and I don't just mean the young ones, to notice she wasn't wearing panties and gather at the side of the dance floor to catch a look."

Blushing, I joined in the conversation. "What do you mean you counseled her—on the spot or later?" This prompted my colleagues to roar with laughter at my poor choice of words and caused me to be even more embarrassed than ever. All I could think of was my daughters and hoped they had better sense than this woman. "Come to think of it, I'm remembering some advice I got from a mentor—you can't call yourself an HR Professional until you've had to tell someone to wear underwear to work."

"You never heard that from me," said Jason as he went on to explain since the party was on the weekend, he'd called her in to his office on Monday morning to talk with her about her choice of dress for a company event. She wasn't a young woman—not that age had anything to do with the issue. She was adamant and didn't think what she'd worn was inappropriate. It was a party and she wore what she always wore when she went out to the clubs on weekends.

Jason told her company social events were an extension of the workplace and while some may call for more festive or casual attire, wearing undergarments was expected, just like in the office.

"That assumes she wore underwear to work," I said having finally regained my composure.

"That was the interesting thing about her," Jason replied. "She was always dressed professionally, almost conservatively, in the office so this was a total departure for her."

Ellen Cooper was sitting directly across from Jason and looking very intently at him. You could almost hear the wheels spinning in her head. "Jason, doesn't the research show it's best to have someone of the same gender have sensitive conversations like the one you had with this woman?"

"Generally, I would, Ellen. But I didn't want to delay or risk someone else saying something to her first. There weren't many women in the office that particular morning. I had a good rapport with her and was confident it would go well, and it did."

Well, this certainly took the discussion in an interesting direction. How can organizations, and in particular HR, deal with employees' total lack of professional judgment?

As he offered refills to everyone, David said, "You know, it seems to me anyone who hasn't worked in HR has no idea of the kinds of things we deal with on a daily basis. One minute I'm in a strategic planning meeting with the CEO and the next, I'm counseling an employee about what's appropriate to wear to work—makes your head spin! Maryanne, when you arrived you said you had something you wanted to share."

"You know the book we're always threatening to write—the one with all the crazy things people do at work. Well, just as I was leaving my office to come here—even had my coat on—I got dragged down the hall by one of the admins. Gayle motioned me to follow her to a workstation at the end of a long corridor. As we got close to the office of one of our executives who's out of town at a conference, I heard a noise that sounded a lot like snoring. It was strange. I could hear the snoring but didn't see anyone at the workstation. Gayle and I shared a look and sort of tiptoed away from the desk. I asked her what she thought, and she was pretty sure the executive's assistant was sleeping under her desk. I didn't want to startle or embarrass anyone, so I asked Gayle to please go back and check to make sure nothing was wrong—that she wasn't ill."

As I paused, Ellen asked, "What did you find out?"

"Gayle looked under the desk and saw the admin was just waking up, so she helped her to her desk chair. Apparently, she is part of a carpool that leaves Indiana at 4:30 each morning to get here by 7 am. She was so exhausted and wanted to rest for a moment. She didn't want to use

What's Wrong with People?

the couch in her boss' office or the one in the women's lounge because she didn't think she'd fall so deeply asleep. She just needed a quick nap."

Ellen was glancing around at everyone. "I try to understand people's motivation, but I'm frequently surprised. Why would someone commute that far each day? I've heard people talk about living far away from work for the *quality of life* when they get home. But, if you are in a van pool or worse, driving yourself four hours a day, do you have any quality of life?"

"I agree," I said. "And, some people can work from home a few days a week, but generally not an administrative assistant—she needs to be on site. I'd love to try to find her a job closer to home, but we don't have any administrative offices in her area. Something to discuss with the HR team at our next staff meeting."

Linda looked up from her notepad and put her pen down. "I heard something very similar recently. The owner of a startup apparently fired this young man on the spot when he found him sleeping under his desk. The young man got defensive saying 'I'm on my lunch hour—the allotted 60 minutes I'm given. I took 10 minutes to eat my lunch then set the alarm on my phone to wake me in another 50 minutes in time to return to work.' The person who told me this asked if I thought the owner was wrong."

Jason made a good point. Did the owner ever consider if there was a medical reason—or some other reasonable explanation—for his napping?

"Speaking of books, Maryanne," said David, "Early in my career, someone told me I'd have a book of stories in my head before long. For example, when I worked at the school district, we had an issue with, and I can only hope you will forgive me for bringing this up, but it was flatulence."

Jason wasn't going to let this go without a dig toward David. With a huge smile on his handsome face, he said "David, this better be good. I've never heard you even hint at something so earthy."

David took it in stride. "Well, one day I had a group of six women waiting for me when I arrived at the office. I mean, they didn't even give me time to hang up my coat before they rushed into my office and all started talking at once. They were all African American women who worked in a small office on the sixth floor. I honestly couldn't remember now what they did, but they all worked together and were supervised by a Caucasian woman who had been with the school district for years. I had never heard any complaints about her management style, but it was obvious something was up, so I asked the women if they could slow down and offered them seats around the conference table in my cramped office. Once seated, they all looked at one woman who apparently would be the spokesperson. She told me there was only one other person in their office except for their supervisor, and it was a white man. They all worked in one room with desks lined up, but he was in a corner of the room with a high partition around him, and this didn't seem fair to them since they all had the same job duties. She said they'd complained to the supervisor that he not only farted all the time but ate at his desk and left food all over the place and the supervisor's solution was to give him private space. Why was he being treated differently?"

"I told them I would need to speak to the supervisor and promised to get back to them that day. Then, I called the supervisor and asked her to come to my office."

I know it doesn't sound very professional, but we were all laughing by now and David understood we all needed some comic relief from time to time—people can make you tired. We pulled ourselves together and let him continue.

The supervisor readily admitted she had requested a partition be brought into the office in an attempt to separate him from the women. "He's a pig," she said, "and I know his behavior—especially the smell—was highly offensive to the others in the office. I thought I was helping."

"I asked her if she'd ever talked with him about it, and she said she'd been too embarrassed and didn't want to escalate it to HR. I told her she should have worked with the employee relations staff on this because now we potentially had a discrimination issue—namely perceived preferential treatment of the white man—on top of the other issues he has."

Looking around the table, I saw understanding nods. "I had a similar situation years ago and checked with our family doctor. She suggested that the individual have a complete physical as most likely there was a medical reason for the flatulence. I was really uncomfortable to start the conversation, but it turned out my doctor was exactly right. The employee had no idea—at least that's what he said. He saw his doctor and in a short time period, all was well."

"Wish my situation had been so easily resolved," David said. "I called the man into my office along with the supervisor and told him he had to clean up his act. If you can imagine, while we were in my tiny office, he, as they say, let one loose, and I nearly gagged. He said he was quitting his job that day, and we let him leave. I had a counseling session with the supervisor about how she'd handled the situation. She did a good job of repairing her relationship with the women in the office and took away the partition."

We talked for a few more minutes about the challenges of our HR world. I shared an experience I bet every HR person has had in some form some time in their career—a male manager coming to me to say a woman in his department had terrible body odor and he couldn't bring himself to talk to her. It was an *HR issue*. I assured him it wasn't but took pity on him since his department was all men except for the woman in question. I talked with her privately, and she said she didn't understand it as she showered daily and used deodorant. We sent her for a physical, and it turned out it was a medical issue. She thanked me for being so kind and gentle with her. It reminded me how important it is for HR professionals to be authentic and caring in these situations—it goes a long way but takes courage. Also, while HR shouldn't take over a manager's responsibility, sometimes a little distance is important when you are dealing with such personal issues.

Stephanie suddenly shrugged. "The issue I struggle with far too often is not body odor, but someone wearing too much perfume or other scents. We try to discourage wearing perfume to work, but then there are scented hair sprays and lotions. We even had an issue with an employee who was so allergic to scents she demanded we put in a policy that everyone had to use unscented laundry detergent and fabric softener. And when I say demanded, I mean it. We ended up moving her to a different part of the building and installing air cleaning units to keep her happy."

Drumming her fingers on the table, Ellen chimed in. "Ladies and gentlemen, let's not forget the communal refrigerators in our lunchrooms so people can bring their lunch if they want to. We always tell people to put their name on their food containers and to be sure not to leave things in the refrigerator too long. But it appears we have an issue with food theft. Recently, a number of people have come to me reporting they left something from their lunch the day before and when they go to get it the following day, it's gone. One guy told me he was going to put something nasty in a sandwich to see if anyone would take it and maybe that would stop the thief."

I threw up my hands. "I know I say this all the time but what's wrong with people? Why don't they understand this is really stealing even if it is just someone's leftovers?"

There was a collective sigh around the room as we discussed ways to resolve this issue, like putting cameras in the lunchroom, but didn't come up a perfect solution. It appears some people don't understand boundaries.

David brought us back to where we started and asked us what we thought of his approach to dealing with the woman who wasn't wearing underwear to work. We all agreed that bringing in the female director to talk with her was a good solution. Then he asked what we thought about perhaps updating the dress code in the employee handbook to specify underwear was to be worn to work. The groups consensus was it could be a challenge enforcing it.

As I was driving home after a very thought-provoking meeting, I couldn't help but focus on what an interesting world we live and work in. My peers are all highly intelligent, successful professionals with advanced degrees and what did we talk about today? We talked about employees behaving badly in the workplace. People challenge us every day. I don't know what tomorrow will bring but no doubt, I'll say *what's wrong with people?* at least once.

CHAPTER 8

What's the Problem?

The voice on the message was hushed. "Someone's doing drugs in the downtown Indianapolis restaurant. I saw him snatch it myself—snatched up a packet that fell out of his pants pocket—shoved it into his backpack—closed his locker quickly. I know this guy's doing drugs. The company better *do* something."

"That's it? No name, no details. Just a *tip* that we have a potential drug user on our hands?" I said turning in my chair to face Valerie London, our General Counsel, who was sitting across the table from me with her left hand propping up her head. She had just played an anonymous message which was left on the Employee Ethics Line—our confidential incident reporting system—early this morning, at about 1:00 am.

Valerie let out an audible sigh as she put down her phone. "They don't give courses in mindreading in law school. I don't know why I listen to these messages before I get to the office. I was cooling down from my workout at the gym this morning. It was an impulse to check messages."

"And I thought they taught lawyers to be omniscient, so you'd know absolutely everything."

"You should know better being married to an attorney," she said, the corners of her mouth curling up. "But frankly, let's look at what we do know. There's a reference to this guy, *his* pants pocket, *his* backpack, and *his* locker, so the alleged perpetrator is probably a male. The caller allegedly saw some kind of packet fall out of his pocket and assumed what it contained, but we don't *know* what was in the packet. We don't know if it was drugs."

"Maybe it was stolen diamonds," I laughed. "So, we know we have *a* problem, we just don't know exactly what the problem is—making it harder to address."

"Afraid so, Maryanne."

"I hate to sound cynical, but whenever we get these anonymous calls placing blame on other employees, I can't help but wonder if the caller has some sort of vendetta against the other person."

"What makes you say that, Maryanne?"

"There have been some employee relations issues at this store before. Being close to the university, we hire so many college students, particularly as wait staff. We've had resentment towards them from the kitchen staff. The mention of a backpack is the only indication it could be a student, but that's not enough. Just like the reference to a packet isn't enough to suspect drugs are the issue."

This was one of those perplexing situations where we couldn't rule anything or anyone out. We had no evidence of any wrongdoing.

"I'd love to know what the caller expects us to *do*," I continued. "Drug test everyone at the restaurant on the basis of reasonable suspicion?

We were very careful when we designed the program that a reasonable suspicion drug test had to be based on specific and observed behavior or performance indicators."

"That was such a good design, Maryanne. Not only for legal issues, but for morale issues as well. I was certainly glad to hear it when I joined Kings." Her tone softening, Valerie continued, "Did I ever tell you about the professional services firm I once worked for? They provided IT and electronic tech support for the government, including the military. We were a subcontractor on a project located at an Army base. Our employees worked in a space adjacent to a machine shop with a changing area for the machinists and mechanics. A bag of marijuana was found in a laundry bin outside the changing area. It could have been anyone's. The prime contractor ordered all employees working in the building to be drug tested within two days. When I asked about the basis for the test, the project director said it was reasonable suspicion. When I protested, he said we were bound to their conditions. Turned out their employees were covered by a union contract, so the drug testing never took place—it didn't meet the reasonable suspicion standard. To be on the safe side, the HR director and I flew down to meet with our 20 or so employees. We were both concerned about employee morale, especially since it was hard to recruit in that location."

I pulled my chair closer to the table. "Valerie, that was close. How did the employees react?"

"Trip paid off. The employees had heard the rumors about drug testing. They appreciated our concern and hearing from us directly."

I was glad to hear Valerie's concern about employee morale. With our former General Counsel, it was always first and foremost whether or not we'd be sued. It was one of the reasons he didn't last long. He saw everything as a legal issue and not a business issue, much less a people issue. Valerie, on the other hand, quickly takes command of every situation with her common-sense approach, especially when dealing with employee issues. It's a refreshing change from other general counsels and attorneys I've worked with, and that includes my husband, Jack.

"Valerie, in this instance, we don't know where to begin investigating. We don't know if it was a kitchen employee—cook or dishwasher—someone on wait staff, or someone else. This anonymity makes fact finding impossible."

Valerie nodded in agreement as she looked at her empty coffee cup. I got up, opened the door, and looked for Ryan Anderson, who'd apparently stepped away. With that, Kyle Greene spotted me and walked up. "Maryanne, Ryan's working with Leslie Hernandez on some reports in the conference room. Can I get anything for you, ma'am?"

Leslie Hernandez is responsible for our HR information system and tracking all necessary and relevant data about our employees—particularly data for payroll and employee benefits. Ryan, the youngest member of our HR team, loves helping her, especially when it comes to designing reports. I suspect Leslie is creating a career path for him, and I'm delighted.

"Thanks, Kyle. Why don't you join us? Valerie can bring you up to speed on something while I get us more coffee."

Valerie gave Kyle a quick summary of the issue we'd been discussing. He asked just the right questions—had we ever had any incidents with drug use on the job in the past and how were they handled.

"Kyle," I replied, "Since I've been here, we've never had direct observation of people using drugs or alcohol on the job. Those are the easiest to spot. We did have a situation once where a bag of pot was discovered in a locker."

Valerie raised an eyebrow and asked sharply, "When? How was it discovered?"

"Relax. This was way before your time here, Valerie. There was an unsecured locker in a changing room in one of the restaurants. The lock was broken. When the employee went to open the door at the end of his shift, the baggie fell out. Three other people saw it. It was at the end of a busy dinner shift. The shift manager was called to the changing room and overreacted. He accused the employee right away and terminated him on the spot. I got calls from both of them the next day."

Kyle's eyes grew wide. "What happened next?" His curiosity was one of his strong and endearing traits.

I described how I had to talk the manager down. He was pretty inflexible in his thinking and insistent he was well within his rights as a manager to terminate the employee immediately. I had to explain that while there appeared to be a policy breach, we didn't have enough information to know who the culprit was. The employee was adamant it was not his pot—someone must have placed it there. He knew for several days the lock was broken, but he hadn't reported it to the shift manager. He claimed someone else knew about the broken lock and must have planted it there. We allowed the employee to continue working while we investigated. We talked to everyone who worked on the shift during that week—the time the lock was broken. Everyone denied knowing the lock was broken and no one admitted to observing anyone placing the bag into the locker.

"Because it was all circumstantial, we weren't able to prove anything nor take any severe disciplinary action. We did give the employee a written warning about breaching facility and security procedures—broken locks and lockers are supposed to be reported immediately. And we counseled the shift manager who was new, verbally and in writing, about never immediately terminating anyone without all the facts. He got the message."

"Did you believe the employee, that the pot wasn't his?" said Kyle.

"I never really dwelled on it. He'd been a good employee—no prior issues."

Kyle brushed his hair away from his face. "Would we react differently today with marijuana being more acceptable and states loosening laws about it?"

Valerie leaned forward, about to protest, but I quickly jumped in. "Kyle, it was, and still is, a violation of our policy to have controlled substances on the premises, unless they are obtained with a valid prescription. It's the same reason we don't allow employees to bring alcohol to work—or be intoxicated. It's a potential safety issue. As a follow up we held mandatory training for the entire restaurant, starting with that shift, on our key policies and procedures, substance abuse policy, drug testing policy, and safety and security."

"Any other dark tales I didn't know about?" sighed Valerie, her head in her hand.

"Yes, right before you joined us. Right here in the corporate office. We had our very own cokehead. I won't tell you which department, but it wasn't HR or legal. The department had a new manager who was very street smart, very savvy. She started to notice some signs in this particular employee's behavior making her suspicious, so she began paying more attention."

"Like what?" Kyle asked.

"Frequent breaks. Disappearances. Long lunches. One time she went looking for him to get some information. When she asked him where he'd been, he became very irritated. Half an hour later, he was ecstatic as he walked into her office with the report she needed. His sporadic work patterns along with changes in mood and behavior led to the decision to refer him for a medical evaluation and external counseling.

"So, what *was* the problem?" Valerie wanted to know.

"Well, he entered a rehabilitation program for thirty days. The first day he came back, we met with him and went over expectations. He went to lunch and returned three hours later. When his manager confronted him, she saw a packet of cocaine in his shirt pocket. We terminated him for having an illegal substance at work. His response, 'I can't believe it took you this long to fire me.'"

Listening to these tales, Kyle shook his head. "They don't teach you how to deal with these issues in school. I never read these things in a textbook. You can't even find the answer in a policy all the time—you can only look to them for guidance."

"Yes, Kyle," I said. "Judgment and common sense are what you often rely on. In this situation there has to be imagination and creativity too."

Kyle's eyes were growing wider. "Getting back to Indianapolis," he continued, "if there'd been an accident, we could consider post-accident drug testing—which gives me an idea."

"Yes," I said, "except we still don't know who or what is involved. But what's your idea?"

Valerie looked puzzled, but before she could say anything, Kyle held up his hand. "Hear me out, Valerie. We could look at the accident records for the downtown Indianapolis restaurant—this year's as well as the past three years' records—look for any trends. Maybe do a quick comparison to other restaurants in the region. With some hard data, we could request a safety inspection."

"Yes," I jumped in. "If the data doesn't support it, perhaps we could request a safety and security audit. Great thinking, Kyle." Turning to Valerie who was nodding in agreement, I continued. "Either way, I could send Kyle along with someone from security, claiming it's a development opportunity for him. This would give him a chance to get in there and observe. He could inquire about the general employee climate. I doubt if we are going to get to the root issue behind this anonymous call, but we might gain some insights."

"And do follow up training like you did in the broken lock situation," suggested Kyle.

"Let's not get ahead of ourselves, Kyle," said Valerie. "It's all going to depend on what, if anything, we find out. But it's a good idea to keep in mind. Maryanne, do you think Mike Foxwell will be agreeable to this?"

"Agreeable with our approach of doing a safety audit and assessing the general employee climate? I think so. While Mike's new to his role as district manager, he's always had good instincts when it comes to people issues and welcomed HR's advice. His management team respects him and won't push back on a routine safety and security audit. I think we need to schedule a call with him, Valerie. You need to let him know about the anonymous call, and I need to let him know the approach I'm proposing. He may have some additional thoughts that will help us."

"Good points, Maryanne," said Valerie. "I'll get a call set up with him today. What does your schedule look like?"

"Ironically, it's wide open. No meetings for a change," I said smiling.

"I'll let you know as soon as it's scheduled. We can call him from my office," Valerie said as she rose to leave. Kyle got up as well and said, "I'll start gathering those reports, ma'am."

"Thank you both," I said. "Valerie, I'll see you later."

After they both left, I looked at the clock. It was almost 11:00. By 11:30 Valerie and I were on the phone with Mike. He was interested in seeing the accident reports for all the restaurants in his district and thought an audit was a great idea. In fact, he suggested doing audits in more than just the downtown Indianapolis restaurant, if not right away, soon. I cautioned him about getting too far ahead, explaining I wanted to see what Kyle might uncover.

"I understand, but I'm really concerned about the so-called tip from this anonymous source, though," he said. "When will people understand there is a difference between confidentiality and anonymity?"

Valerie agreed. "Once at another company, I spent over an hour on the phone with a caller who insisted on remaining anonymous and refused to disclose the location of the alleged wrongdoing. He insisted the company promoted the line as being anonymous—we didn't—and said if he revealed where he was calling from, everyone would know he made the call."

"Mike, this is likely one of those calls we can't resolve. As we all know working with people, not all issues are black and white—there's so much grey area. And we're stymied when we don't have any or all the facts. If there really is an issue with drugs in this case, I'm hoping that sending Kyle alerts both the user and the caller to the fact that we take the issue seriously. On the other hand, if this is a hoax or a set-up, we're still sending a message to the accuser—calls to the Ethics Line aren't taken lightly."

"I understand, Maryanne. It's just so frustrating. I don't know how you deal with this all the time," Mike replied.

"Well, I did make a note to talk to Nicolle Livingston on my employment development and training team about revamping our annual training for the ethics and incident reporting systems this year. We need to stress that if employees have the expectation of resolution, they've got to be open and disclose details and be willing to participate in an investigation. Transparency works both ways." Valerie nodded in agreement motioning to me she wanted to be included.

"Maryanne, how soon do you think Kyle can have those accident reports to me? And when do you think he can do the audit?"

"He's working on the reports now. I'll have him follow up with you directly to coordinate the details of the audit. And I'll let him know it's a priority."

"Thanks, Maryanne. Look forward to hearing from him," said Mike before hanging up the phone.

CHAPTER 9

Too Close for Comfort

I could hear my cell phone buzzing in my purse as I walked from the train station to the office. Entering the building, I pulled it out and saw I'd missed a call from Allison Walters, the young HR professional whom I was informally mentoring. I sent her a quick text—Will call shortly.

Once I was settled in my office, I listened to her message. Allison was talking very fast, something she does when she's upset or nervous. I tried to listen carefully, but the message was breaking up. All I could understand was something about her sister. *I hope everything's okay* I thought as I hit the call back button.

"Oh Marianne," she gasped. "Thanks so much for calling back so quickly." I could tell Allison was still upset.

"Marianne, remember I told you about my sister Suzanne? She graduated from college last spring and went to work for a research company."

"Yes, I do, Allison. Take a deep breath before you continue. Sounds like something's wrong."

I could hear a big sigh on the other end. "Her supervisor's a guy, probably in his early 30s. He acts awkward—almost geeky—around people, but he keeps doing things that creep her out. She's not sure if it's sexual harassment. It's all very weird, and most of this stuff happens when it's just the two of them working together."

Classic situation I thought. Before I could say anything, Allison continued.

"But it gets even worse. She told her boyfriend, Joe, who's really pissed. So, Joe told his buddy, Luke, who works at Suzanne's company, and Luke said Suzanne needed to report it, but she just wants to find another job. Then, when Luke went into work the next day, he told his supervisor, Eva, what Suzanne was going through. Eva said she had to report it to HR, because she had notice of the behavior—she *had* to take some action, even though the matter was outside her department. She told Luke he'd done the right thing by telling her, suggested he talk with Suzanne, and said she'd wait 24 hours before talking to HR."

"Did Luke talk to Suzanne about it?"

"Yes, but Maryanne she's so upset. She thinks her boyfriend betrayed her trust, but Luke explained to her he's really upset her supervisor's acting like this too—socially inept or not, he said it was just wrong." Allison was talking fast again.

"Time for another deep breath, Allison. When did this happen?"

"Just this week. Today's the day Luke's supervisor is going to talk to HR. Suzanne just called me all upset. It turns out her supervisor is out sick today, and she doesn't know what to do. Maryanne, what should I tell her?"

Allison's voice was quivering, and I could tell she was on the verge of tears. I sensed she was very upset not only because this was happening to her younger sister, but because Suzanne looked up to her *and* turned to her with this problem because she was an HR professional. She was struggling because she didn't know how to advise Suzanne.

"Allison, when you're so close to a situation, it's hard to be objective. Can we conference Suzanne into this call so I can talk to her directly?"

"No," said Allison. "I think it would upset her more to talk to someone she doesn't know. Can you give me some ideas of what I need to tell her?"

"I've seen a lot of these situations in my day, and these are rarely isolated incidents unless there is a uniquely clueless person out there. Suzanne needs to go to HR herself to report this. If she talks to me first, it will be a good dry run. She can get past her emotions with me and be better prepared to give her HR department all of the facts."

"I don't know, Maryanne, but I'll try."

Allison put me on hold while she tried to call Suzanne. It took a few attempts, but she finally managed to get Suzanne on the line and introduced us. I asked Suzanne if she was in a place where she could talk confidentially. She was. Since her supervisor was out sick, she'd left the building and was sitting in her car. To build some rapport and trust, and to calm her down, I shared my background and explained I've had lots of experience with bizarre behavior at work. I even told her a funny story not related to harassment, and she let out a small laugh.

Good, she's getting comfortable, I thought. I asked her to tell me when this behavior began. I wasn't surprised it was shortly after she'd started working there. It was subtle at first, but strange, like the day he approached her at her cubicle—no one was around. He asked her to stand up and turn around. She did, and then he abruptly turned and walked away.

Then, one evening when she was leaving, he passed her in the hall, dropped some papers and asked her to pick them up. He moved behind her as she bent over like he was checking out her butt. She thrust the papers at him and quickly left. Nothing else happened for a while, not until this week. They were working late this time, and he came into her cubicle to look at something on her computer. He came up behind her and put his face so close to her ear she could feel his breath, muttering something about her earrings, like he was paying her a compliment. It made her very uncomfortable, and she pushed her chair away.

"What happened next?" I asked.

"I told him I had to go, shut down my laptop, got my things, left and called my boyfriend," Suzanne said. "Maryanne, he's just so... So icky. I just want to forget this and find a new job."

"Suzanne, I know this is intimidating for you, and I'm sorry you're having such a bad experience on your first job out of college. But it's so important you speak up. It's the only way any problem will be solved. For all you know, this guy's some sort of serial harasser. If he's doing this to you, he may have done it before, or still be doing it, to other women. As someone who's been in business and HR for as long as I have, trust me, this behavior has got to be stopped. Now, you did a great job of describing what happened to me over the phone. Do you think you're ready to go back into the building and meet with HR? Remember, if Luke's supervisor has already given them some information, they won't be surprised. But they need to hear this firsthand from you."

"Yes, after talking with you, Maryanne, I do think I can talk to HR. And thanks for listening to me." She hesitated for a moment before continuing, "Huh, I never thought he might be doing this to other women. That makes a big difference. Come to think of it, I just remembered I have heard some rumors about him. I was just upset about how it was affecting me. I was struggling to meet some deadlines—that's why I was working late."

He was throwing her off her guard. How predictable, I thought.

"Well, I'm glad this helped. Be sure to tell HR everything—including the rumors you heard. They may have some substance. And please let me know what happens."

"I will," I heard both Allison and Suzanne say in unison.

Around 4:30 pm Ryan came in to tell me he had Allison on hold for me. It seems when Suzanne went back in the building and got herself together, she went to HR and told them everything she told me about her supervisor. HR asked her if she was aware of anyone else having a similar problem. She said she wasn't sure but shared the rumors she'd heard. HR promised they would do an investigation. I told Allison HR probably wanted to determine if there was a pattern of this type of behavior.

"I promise I'll keep you posted if I learn anything else," Allison said. She sounded very relieved.

* * *

Ellen Cooper is hosting the networking meeting this month. As everyone was getting a light snack, Ellen mentioned it's time for her company's annual sexual harassment training. There was a collective sigh from the group. The sentiment didn't have to be spoken—all the training in the world is no guarantee bad behavior will stop.

"Right?" Ellen said. "I'm trying to come up with a hook to grab their attention at the start and get them engaged."

"Well, I heard an interesting situation recently," I said. As everyone was settling in their seats, I shared my conversation with Allison and Suzanne.

"Did you ever hear what finally happened?" asked Ellen.

"The supervisor was terminated. After the investigation, HR got back to Suzanne and told her they were able to corroborate all the rumors she heard. The time he was caught standing at the stairwell apparently up-skirting women walking up and down the stairs. The time he told a woman she had something on her blouse, moved close to her and attempted to brush it off. The time he approached a woman and asked what color panties she was wearing. Apparently, each woman confronted him at the scene—told him to never do it again. He stopped the behavior with each of them individually but found someone else to target. Meantime, these women each figured out ways to avoid him. They adapted coping strategies but didn't speak up or report the behavior. No one knew to investigate until Suzanne came forward."

What a valuable lesson to learn so early in your working career," Ellen said. "Someone thinks they've handled the problem, but they don't realize it continues to fester elsewhere."

"That's exactly what I told Suzanne, and it's the message we need to get across—to all young, working people, especially women. Find the courage to speak up. And we've *got* to support them when they do speak up. It's the only way the problem will be solved," I said.

I noticed David Morgan had a big grin on his face. "What's. So. Funny?" I snapped.

"Sorry, Maryanne. I was just thinking I bet Suzanne's supervisor got all defensive about his actions when he was confronted and claimed he thought he was just being friendly."

The floodgates opened for everyone's sexual harassment stories.

"I have an absolute favorite," said Ellen. "I was asked to investigate a harassment claim for another business unit while the HR Director was on a medical leave. And you all know how I'd rather be working with data. Anyway, among the dumb things this manager did was to send a text message to one young woman on his team that said, and I quote: 'Do you like it when I say I think you're sexy?' He couldn't deny it because they had a printout of the message. When I confronted the manager, he responded, 'I was just being playful. I didn't mean anything by it. After all, I can say that I think you're sexy.'"

Linda Goodman stopped doodling in her notebook. "For real? He said that?"

"Yes, he did, Linda. And actually, my first thought was no, no you can't say that—not if you want to keep your job."

Ellen went on to explain this wasn't the only text he'd sent to the same woman. There were a number of them commenting on her looks or something she was wearing. She thought it was odd that he'd text her something that appeared to be a compliment—that's a nice outfit you're wearing today—rather than just tell her. But when he started telling her she looked hot or sexy, that's when she reported it.

Linda stopped adjusting the deep blue scarf she was wearing. "How did you get the printout of the text?"

"The genius not only used his company phone, he sent them to hers, so IT had the record of all the texts he sent. Of course, he kept saying he didn't understand what he did wrong, claiming he was just teasing and wanting to apologize. I suspected he thought he could talk his way out of it with me since I was from a different company unit. I don't have to tell you our harassment training covered the concept of intent versus impact, and I checked the records to make sure he'd attended. He heard the message loud and clear—it's not the intention but the impact the behavior has on others that's a determining factor in harassment."

Waving her pen, Linda said, "Maybe you needed to draw him a picture. Were there other instances of it with anyone else?"

"Not that came to our attention. His admission and the texts were enough data—evidence, I guess—to make a decision to terminate him pretty quickly. The woman was pretty shaken up by the situation, wondering what she'd done wrong."

"And so much for thinking annual training alone is going to stop harassment." I said.

"So true, Maryanne," said Jason Edison. "But back to Ellen's story, and yours, I love it when they're in denial that they did anything wrong."

"Or when it's somehow your fault." said Linda, tapping her fingers on the table.

Jason's head turned toward her so quickly, I thought he was going to suffer whiplash. "Your fault?"

"Yes, my fault, and I'll get to it. Naturally, there's a story coming, Jason. A young woman in her mid-20s didn't want to attend a conference because she had to travel with one of the directors, a man. When I asked her why, she said he was always following her, and didn't I remember him following her to the restroom during a corporate function months earlier, like I was supposed to remember seeing them."

Frowning, Jason said, "Is that why it was your fault?"

"Oh, no. It gets even better," Linda continued, "but in the interest of time, I'll get to the point. She implied he was stalking her, but we learned they'd been having a little fling. After she broke it off and started dating someone closer to her age, he got riled and tried to win her back. This was interesting. When I asked her about the affair with him and if it was consensual, she said it wasn't anyone's business."

David leaned forward. "Then what?"

"The CEO and I confronted the director who admitted he was infatuated with her and crushed when she'd ended the affair, and yes, continued to pursue her. Then he turned to me and said, 'Linda, this is all your fault—you didn't counsel me enough.' That comment just about put the CEO over the edge. He explained there was no room for this type of behavior and advised him we'd be terminating his employment."

Stephanie Packard, who'd been very quiet up till now, slowly turned to Linda and pulled off her reading glasses. "Sooo? Did you apologize to him?" Everyone burst into laughter.

I reached my hand across the table toward Linda. "What happened with the young woman?"

"I tried coaching her hoping she'd see how casual affairs, especially with a manager, can backfire, stressing he was accountable for his behavior. But I sensed she never quite grasped that the lack of boundaries between social and professional relationships played a huge role in the overall problem. She left the company not long after."

Raising his tented fingers to his chin, Jason said, "Think about it. Linda's story is an example of one problem with harassment—it involves human behavior and interaction. Both parties often contribute to bad behavior, and when there are no witnesses those situations get complicated. But sometimes there's other evidence."

"Such as?" I said tilting my head in his direction.

"Let's talk physical evidence and sexual assault. This happened while I was working out of a New York office. At first, the behavior was innocent, though childish. This guy would annoy a particular female co-worker—sit too close in meetings, poke her with paper clips, or jab her arm to get her attention. She repeatedly told him to stop, but he kept it up. Then they went on a business trip to Boston with a group of other employees, and things changed drastically. After dinner, they were the last ones in the elevator. Without warning, he threw her up against the wall and attempted to kiss her. When she resisted and struggled to get free, he put his hands around her neck hard enough to bruise her. Suddenly, the elevator opened on her floor—someone else was getting on—and she managed to get away and run to her room where she sat up all night very upset. In the morning she called HR, and we told her to get on the first train she could and get back."

Jason went on to tell us everyone was alarmed when she arrived in HR's office that August afternoon with a heavy scarf around her neck trying to hide the bruises. This was before every phone had a camera. Luckily, HR had access to a Polaroid camera—if anyone remembers those—used to take employees' pictures for their badges and took pictures of the bruises on her neck. After talking with the company's general counsel and the man's manager, the man was contacted and told to be in the office first thing the next morning for a meeting. He never suspected the meeting would be about him. He denied any wrongdoing claiming she was a willing participant. When confronted with the pictures, he said she liked it rough. That's when the general counsel advised him that the hotel had already been contacted, pulled the security tape from the halls, and identified the person getting on the elevator—a hotel employee who would serve as a witness. He agreed to go quietly.

"And the woman? What happened to her?" said Ellen.

"We offered her time off if she wanted to speak to a counselor, and the general counsel told her she could file an assault complaint, but she'd have to return to Boston to do so. She was so grateful we took immediate action and he was gone."

Stephanie hesitated, a pensive expression forming on her face. "Has anyone ever been in a situation where the company found the harasser was at fault but didn't fire them?"

"Really, why would you want to keep them around? A company's just asking for trouble if they don't get rid of them," said Ellen.

"That's a tough one. I'd say it depends," said David as he leaned back in his chair. "I've never been in a situation where keeping the perpetrator of harassment was an option, but one of my team members once was. Seems this high-level director from a South American country was accused of sexually harassing three women who reported to him. The behavior was apparently pretty bad."

"Details, David, details," Stephanie laughingly pleaded.

"I'm getting to them," David said.

The behavior he went on to describe was unbelievable. The director would greet the women almost every day by kissing them. At first, they didn't think much of it recognizing it wasn't unusual in his South American culture for people to exchange kisses on the cheek. But when his tongue started finding its way to their lips and when he started making comments on how nice they smelled—not casual comments on their perfume, but attempts to nuzzle their neck when he walked up behind them—they requested a meeting with HR and the general counsel. On the morning of that meeting, he approached one of the women and started stroking her arm commenting how much he liked the material on her lab coat. As he continued to stroke her, he said the material was so soft just like he imagined her body was.

"And they didn't fire him?" everyone else said in unison.

"Apparently not," said David. "It was a difficult decision, but leadership determined they really needed his expertise and background. It was a research and development firm working on a new product. He had specialized knowledge he gained in his home country and a unique skill set no other scientist in the world possessed. The company had spent thousands to recruit him and needed his expertise to get the product to market—a product projected to make them hundreds of millions of dollars."

David paused and took a sip of water. "They immediately did damage control—removed him from his management role, limited his contact with the women as best they could, and put him on a really short leash. He had required weekly sessions with the general counsel, who kept an eagle's eye on him. However, the women still had to have some interaction with him, and one-by-one, they resigned, which was a loss. At least the leadership didn't take the boys-will-be-boys attitude this time, but the decision did have a strong negative impact on all the women in the company—something that probably hadn't been anticipated when it was made."

"Still," said Ellen. "No woman should *ever* have to be subjected to that type of behavior at work."

David almost bolted from his chair. "Hold on, Ellen. No *person* should ever have to be subjected to this type of disgraceful behavior. I'm not judging that company's decision. None of us have all the facts to do so. But with all due respect, men aren't the only ones demonstrating bad behavior at work."

"Point well taken, David," Stephanie interjected, shooting a puzzled look in my direction. I'd never seen David quite this upset, nor Ellen this emotional. Stephanie quickly turned to Ellen. "Remember the case we heard about at that conference recently?"

"Indeed, I do," Ellen responded. "And sorry David," she said sheepishly.

Stephanie purposefully spoke in a steady, low-pitched voice before any more emotion bubbled up. "This VP of HR from a manufacturing company told us about one of their sales directors who was a terrible manager. The classic—*he is great at sales and with customers, has some practical experience, so let's make him a manager*—scenario. But…when it came to managing people, not so great. Overcompensated by micromanaging. He had six female sales reps on his team, all pretty young—late 20s, early 30s—and single. Their complaints about his management style fell on deaf ears because of his success in landing new accounts."

As Stephanie stopped to take a sip of coffee, Ellen joined in. "And they were convinced he was harassing them. They also complained he'd eavesdrop on their conversations about their weekends and after-work activities. According to them, he was attempting to learn more about their sex lives. It was a reach."

"Yes, it was," continued Stephanie. "Well, it came to a head at a mandatory, after-hours networking event he scheduled. He made the mistake of drinking too much and the women took advantage of it. They snatched his phone and one of them snapped a photo of her bare midriff—you could see the tops of her panties and the bottom of her breasts, but nothing more."

Cocking his head, David said in a devilish, bad-boy voice, "Was she wearing a bra?"

I was relieved when everyone burst out laughing. The tension had been released.

Stephanie waved her hand at him dismissing the remark. "They sent the photo to people in the corporate office. HR investigated the entire situation, the micromanaging, the harassment, and the photo. They concluded strained relationships were making the work environment difficult, but he hadn't harassed anyone. As far as the eavesdropping went, they spoke openly, and loudly, about their personal activities, and yes, sometimes descriptions got, shall we say, intimate and graphic. Others in the office said no one could help overhearing them. In fact, they were probably guilty of harassing him."

"So, what happened to him, Stephanie," I asked.

"They got a coach to work with him on his management style. He did very well with the coach's guidance and has been a model employee ever since. The women continued to find things to complain about, but his behavior remained above board. Eventually all the women left."

"I hate to say this," I said, "but these situations we've been discussing seem tame compared to the sensational stories that make the news."

"Yeah, the companies that throw money at problems hoping the harassment will go away?" said Linda, looking up from her notebook. "Do they realize they're just increasing the cost of doing business and not solving anything? And they're risking alienating the public and their advertisers."

"Look," said David. "We all know sexual harassment is about control and the abuse of power. I welcome any of you ladies to disagree with me, but I'm sure many of the women in these sensational stories—even the stories we never read or hear about—take a settlement because they want these nightmares they're living to be over. They want to move on with their lives."

"I don't disagree, David," said Linda. "These situations, if drawn out, can be emotionally draining on the women and their families. But think of the story that started the evening, Suzanne's supervisor—the serial harasser. The other women used avoidance tactics to cope which isn't unusual. While the story ended positively, many of those women suffered along the way. And many situations like it never get resolved."

Stephanie bolted up in her chair. "What so many people don't understand, and frankly, I get tired of explaining it whenever these stories hit the news, is that women often don't speak up because they're afraid. They're afraid they won't be taken seriously or worse, lose their jobs. They can suffer financial consequences. If the other women in Suzanne's company had all spoken up earlier, even collectively, that company likely would have taken action sooner. There's safety in numbers.

"Think about this," Linda said. "Those two younger men in Maryanne's story, the boyfriend and his buddy, they were aware enough to be upset by that supervisor's behavior. That probably wouldn't have happened in the early days of any of our careers. It may be baby steps, but it's progress."

There was a collective pause as if everyone was reflecting on events they've dealt with.

"There is one positive thing that comes from those sensational headlines," I said. "It brings the problem of harassment to the front of everyone's mind. No question the problem exists—no persists—but we have made progress recognizing it can't be ignored and placed in a corner somewhere. To Linda's point, kudos to Suzanne's male friends. But it's only going to be stopped when employers—and the bad actors—are made accountable."

"And," said David, "when organizations stop protecting the so-called valued employees—the ones they deem as the untouchables."

"Indeed," Ellen said. "We could continue this discussion all night, but I think it's time to wrap up. We can explore these issues another time."

"Another month, another set of issues. We're never at a loss for a topic to talk about," said Jason. "It's good we don't set a firm agenda for these discussions," he said as he rose to leave. "See everyone next month."

CHAPTER 10

The Master Made Me Do It

"Great, Kyle, you're here. Did you tell her yet that Bobby Rogers wants her fired?" Judy Marshall exclaimed.

It was as if Judy had suddenly materialized in my office. Kyle was standing in front of my desk, beginning to brief me about something and suddenly there was Judy. I took a deep breath and thought, *what the heck is going on?*

"I just walked in before you did and was about to tell Maryanne that Bobby's in an uproar," he responded to Judy.

After being on vacation for two weeks, I was grateful for the opportunity to get into the office early this Monday morning to catch up before the staff arrived. But promptly at 8:00, Kyle appeared in my doorway. The papers he was holding didn't go unnoticed.

"Great, you're back Maryanne. How was vacation, ma'am?" he said as he'd walked in. "Ralph, wanted you to get these first thing this morning.

You missed some excitement Friday afternoon. I didn't want to contact you and ruin the end of your vacation."

Now Judy was talking excitedly over Kyle and was saying something about St. Louis. I signaled time out to both of them, "Who does Bobby want fired? Me?" as I motioned to Kyle to hand over the papers he was holding.

Judy paused, then took a deep breath. "Sorry, I guess we did rush you a bit first thing, Maryanne. But Ralph does want to meet as soon as possible this morning. And we have to brief Valerie London as well. She was at a meeting with outside counsel Friday afternoon. And no, it's not you Bobby wants to fire. By the way, how was your vacation?"

"Thanks for asking. Our vacation was wonderful. Now would you both go get some coffee and give me a few minutes to read this?"

As they walked out, I looked closer at the papers Kyle had handed me. It was a letter which I assumed was a demand letter from an attorney. No wonder Valerie, our General Council, needed to be involved. But the letter was from a mediator claiming to represent a waitress, Bettina Gordon, who worked in one of the St. Louis area restaurants. He was offering to mediate a dispute between Bettina and Kings—specifically, Emil Bruener, the store manager. The letter claimed Bettina was being assigned poor work schedules because she suffers from bipolar disorder and is being harassed by her co-workers who are creating a hostile work environment for her. Certain we would want to avoid a formal charge of discrimination on the basis of Bettina's disability, his letter was an offer to mediate. The final page contained the mediator's fee schedule.

Okay, why all the commotion? This letter is coming from a mediator and not an attorney. I'm certain Valerie will raise her legal eyebrows, but it's not the first time an employee's claimed discrimination. We'll investigate and get to the bottom of this. Oh, wait, Bobby Rogers, the district manager for St. Louis. He reports to Judy, the VP of Food and Beverage. Bobby is very loyal to Kings, but he can be perceived as hard-nosed and hard charging. I sighed, looked at my coffee mug. Empty. I grabbed it and got up. Time for a refill. Kyle and Judy were standing by his office. I motioned toward my office and told them I'd be right there.

I learned from Judy and Kyle that Emil was stunned by the accusations. He called Bobby right away and told him that this waitress acted strangely at times, but no one was aware she was bipolar. She'd been calling in sick a lot, and Emil had documented it. Bobby had tried to call the waitress to schedule a meeting but couldn't reach her. He wants her fired because she's unreliable.

By this time, it was after 8:30. Judy looked up and nodded towards the door. I turned around and saw my assistant, Ryan, standing there.

"Excuse me. Valerie London's looking for you both."

"Thank you, Ryan. Please let Valerie know Judy's in my office with me and ask her to join us. We need to discuss something with her."

When Valerie came in, I let Kyle fill her in on the letter and the mediator's claim. Before he could tell her what happened on Friday, Judy interrupted.

"Bobby wants this waitress gone and soon. It's not just her absenteeism, but she's creating disturbances at the restaurant. She's been counseled and doesn't respond, and he expects things won't improve. Frankly, he may be right."

This was the first I heard of disturbances and was about to say something when Valerie held out her hand signaling Judy to stop and cut her off.

"Hang on a minute, Judy. What kind of disturbances?"

"Uh, he didn't exactly say," Judy responded, a sheepish look forming on her face. It wasn't like her to be quite this agitated nor jump to conclusions.

"Look, Judy," Valerie said calmly, but I sensed she was growing annoyed. "First of all, this letter is nonsense. It's from a mediator who is partial to the employee's story when he's supposed to be neutral, but I'll deal with him later. What's important is our need to investigate this matter—look into these allegations. For starters, we need to clarify that there was no previous knowledge of a disability—that includes anything that might remotely be interpreted as a request for a reasonable accommodation. We need more information about her behavioral issues. Was there a pattern to her absenteeism? What kind of disturbances was she causing? Were they with co-workers, customers, or both? As general counsel, I'll direct the investigation. Kyle can you come up with an investigation plan for me?"

Judy glanced at Kyle, who spoke up. "Valerie, while Bobby was on the phone with us on Friday, I explained if we terminated the waitress now, even with cause, she'd probably claim we discriminated against her because of a medical condition—which we now know about thanks to the mediator—and then retaliated because she complained, making the situation even worse for Kings."

As Valerie nodded in agreement with Kyle, she turned to me and winked. *Yes, we'd both been good mentors to him.*

With everyone briefed, I asked Ryan to call Ralph and find out about a good time to meet. Ryan came back and said Ralph was on his way to my office. Before he arrived, we all agreed to let Valerie be the spokesperson.

"Good morning folks," he said as he walked through the door. Before he could say anything more, Valerie took charge of the conversation. She explained we agreed with Kyle's assessment—we couldn't terminate this woman at least not now with knowledge of her medical condition.

Looking pleased, Ralph gestured toward Kyle. "I wasn't surprised when Kyle told me that on Friday. But as Judy can tell you, Bobby Rogers is really going to bat for his store manager."

I asked Judy what we knew about Emil. She shared he'd been with Kings for three years, is a protégé of Bobby's, and does a great job managing the store. The sales have increased every year since he's been there, and Bobby sees him on track for advancement. "I'm scheduled to go out there on Wednesday. Can Kyle accompany me and do an investigation?"

Kyle looked at me and I shook my head yes. "Put an investigation plan together and have Valerie sign off on it." I was greatly relieved. We had a plan to proceed and Judy's attitude had softened.

Ralph nodded in agreement. "I'll leave it in your capable hands. Just let me know if anything changes. And Judy, let Bobby Rogers know what you're planning and that I'm behind it."

Later that afternoon, Kyle brought me the investigation plan he'd outlined which included people he'd talk to, a list of questions he was prepared to ask, and the documentation he would gather. It was well thought out and when we ran it by Valerie, she agreed.

* * *

Over the next three days, Kyle kept me updated. He told me about the conversation with Emil on Wednesday. It seems Bettina, the waitress, had given him a written request to work the lunch shift to coincide with her children's school schedule—a request Emil was able to honor most of the time. Kyle had asked pointed questions: Did Bettina say or indicate anything about a reasonable accommodation? Did she ever present a doctor's note? How often did he ask her to work a different schedule and when he did, did she ever complain? The answer to all of these questions was no. While he rarely asked her to work a different schedule, sometimes he offered her an additional shift which she usually declined because of her children's school schedule.

Then things took an interesting turn in the discussion. Emil shared Bettina often called in 30 minutes before the start of shift saying she wasn't coming into work leaving the restaurant short-handed. Sometimes she claimed she was sick, but often she gave an excuse that she couldn't work with particular employees—Sonia makes fun of my hair or Rita never smiles at me. She accused Emil of deliberately scheduling her to work with people who he knew picked on her.

And there were instances of erratic behavior. She would greet customers with a big exuberant smile, but by the time she brought their orders, she'd slam down the food on the table. She'd go weeks being just fine, then the erratic behavior would begin again—like the day two weeks ago when she almost dropped a tray of food and then screamed at the busboy who was the one who actually caught it before it fell. Kyle was concerned about this pattern of behavior which had been occurring for a few months. Why were we first hearing about it now? The behavior indicated something was wrong, yet Emil hadn't mentioned it to anyone, not even Bobby. He had considered calling HR or the EAP—employee assistance program, our external resource to help staff members deal with personal issues—but said he just got too busy. On a positive note, Emil did a good job documenting all of her absences and the complaints about her from other employees and the customers. He just hadn't taken any action.

"When you say he hadn't taken any action, Kyle, what do you mean? Did he ever talk to her about the complaints?"

"That's just the thing," said Kyle. "He counselled her on several occasions about the absenteeism and documented each session. He also wrote down a list of the complaints he'd received from customers and co-workers. When I asked how she reacted when he spoke to her about those complaints, he said they mostly happened during the lunch rush. By the time he had a chance to do or say anything, the shift was over, and she was gone. So, he'd write them down, but never get around to talking to her. When I pressed him, Emil confessed he wasn't comfortable confronting her about the complaints."

"What are your next steps? It sounds like you'll have to do more digging than we anticipated."

Kyle planned to review Emil's documentation and talk with Sonia and Rita, the waitresses Bettina complained about along with Fred, the busboy with whom she had an altercation. Judy helped him arrange all the logistics for the interviews including one with Bettina.

"Depending on what I find out, I plan to review my initial findings with Judy in the afternoon. She wants to leave open the possibility of talking with Bettina again on Friday before her shift. Do you want me to call you again tomorrow?"

On Thursday, as expected, Kyle called again to report the day's events. Nothing unexpected came from the interviews with the other waitresses, and they both seemed to have good recall of the events. Rita had witnessed several disturbances with the customers and provided lots of detail. She also heard rumors of Bettina accusing her of *stealing her customers and taking her tips*, probably because Rita often stepped in to smooth things over. It's no wonder she never smiled at Bettina.

As for Sonia, she once suggested Bettina pull her hair back in a clip to keep it from falling in her face at work and Bettina lashed out at her. She also told Kyle she often overheard Bettina make snarky comments to customers which she'd reported to Emil and which he included in his documentation.

Poor Fred, the busboy—he thought he was getting fired. He told Kyle he'd been standing near the pick-up window when he saw Bettina fumbling with a tray of food—trying to get all the plates to balance on it. He asked if she needed help, but she ignored him and turned quickly moving in his direction almost dropping the tray. He reached out and helped her steady it, once again offering help, but she just walked off. After she delivered the meals to the customers, she stormed into the kitchen and started screaming at poor Fred. He called her something nasty under his breath, and he thought someone heard it and reported him. Emil was out on the floor, but one of the cooks witnessed the incident in the kitchen. The cook told him to let Emil know, which he did. And the cook apparently also told Emil about it which was also documented.

"Kyle, tell me how things went with Bettina," I said. "Did you question her about all these incidents?"

He was silent for a moment. "Yes, I did, and she was very defensive. She denied the incidents with Rita and Fred, but Emil corroborated both of their versions. She accused Sonia of always criticizing her and often pulling her hair. She also told me she said she just couldn't work with certain people because they made faces at her behind her back and she was afraid they'd break into her locker and put poison on her things. When I pressed her for more details, she couldn't provide any—no names, nor specific circumstances. I asked her if she ever reported her concerns to Emil. She said no because she couldn't trust him and everyone was against her."

After hearing what Kyle had uncovered, Judy was pretty annoyed with Emil—his procrastination, his failure to reach out to anyone, and his failure to observe the behavioral indicators that there might be a bigger problem. For someone who was so defensive of her team earlier in the week, she now had a different view and opinion. Bobby, too, was surprised to learn all this had been going on.

"I've got to admit, Bobby did quite a turnaround from last Friday, Maryanne. I've never seen him act quite this humbly." Kyle told me.

"Well, he put a lot of faith in Emil and apparently stopped paying attention. What happened next?"

Kyle went on to explain that after lunch they met with Emil at the district office. Judy was ready to read him the riot act, but Kyle calmed her down. They told Emil there was no evidence of discrimination nor retaliation, and we were satisfied the letter was the first evidence we had of Bettina's bipolar disorder. Then Kyle asked him about her outbursts. Emil admitted he was concerned about them but didn't address them with her—didn't know how. That's when Judy explained it was a mistake keeping this information to himself. He should have advised any or all of us—Bobby, herself, Maryanne, or Kyle. We would have supported him. She told him we might have been able to intervene with Bettina sooner and get her help.

My staff and I are constantly reminding our managers that sometimes the issues our employees are struggling with are outside our realm of expertise as business professionals, and we need to turn to health care professionals, such as licensed therapists, who can diagnose mental disorders.

The employee assistance program meets that need. It's a resource where employees can talk confidentially with a therapist about issues in their personal lives that may also be affecting their work.

As if he was reading my mind, Kyle said, "I reminded Emil the EAP is a resource for managers as well as employees and they could have helped him—all of us—confront Bettina in a positive way. Then, surprisingly, Bobby chimed in. He was supposed to just observe, but it worked well. Bobby told Emil he sympathized with his reluctance to confront Bettina, then reminded him none of us in the room were experts in human behavior. That's why we have an employee assistance program."

"Well, it's not surprising. Bobby's been on the receiving end of these conversations, and he's learned to use the EAP as a management resource himself." Then I asked how they left things with Emil and if they planned to speak with Bettina again.

Emil was told this was just an oral counseling, and he was relieved and grateful for all the support. Kyle and Judy would be talking to Bettina the following morning, Friday, before they caught their afternoon flight back to Chicago.

* * *

The meeting with Bettina didn't go well. She was initially unresponsive until Judy began to share Emil's documentation about the disturbances. She denied them and became combative. When Judy said Kings offered its staff an employee assistance program, Bettina lost it. She said it would make her job much easier if everyone would stop making fun of her behind her back and calling her *crazy*. She said she now had proof we thought she was crazy—otherwise why would we offer her the EAP. She started making accusation against everyone and said the company was discriminating against her—the first time she made that allegation—and she was going to fight it. Then she quietly got up, excused herself, and said she had to go.

Judy called Emil and alerted him what had happened. He had the shift on Friday covered in case she didn't come in that day—and she never did show up.

Bettina did come to work on Monday and Tuesday but was a no-show on Wednesday. On Thursday, a charge of discrimination from the Equal Employment Opportunity Commission came to the regional office. As soon as he received it, Bobby emailed a copy to Valerie who called and instructed both Bobby and Emil not to talk to Bettina about the discrimination charge and not to take any action which could be considered retaliatory. Her counsel wasn't necessary. Bettina never returned to work

Valerie learned that the EEOC offered mediation and Bettina requested her mediator be appointed. The EEOC explained the parties didn't get to choose their mediator, so she declined. Several months later, on the day after we were notified the EEOC had dismissed the charge without merit, Ralph called Kyle and me to his office and presented Kyle with a spot bonus of $1,000 for doing such a great job.

"You see, Kyle," he said, "the people side of business used to be a lot easier when my father started Kings. And not as much was known about mental illness back then, so employees didn't always get the best deal."

Kyle looked puzzled, so Ralph continued. "When my father was still running the company, we had a head of accounting, we didn't call them CFOs back then, who was very irritable. We just figured he was better with numbers than with people. The he started acting very unpredictably. Be screaming one moment, charming the next. Coming in late, especially on Monday mornings, or leaving early, especially on Fridays, with no explanation. At first, we all tried to take a friendly approach when dealing with this behavior, but then he started making mistakes on the financial reports and denying he made them. I was managing the Loop store at the time and noticed a pattern of discrepancies with sales reports and payroll. My dad grew concerned but was convinced he wouldn't do anything to hurt the company. Finally, when he failed to make a tax deposit resulting in stiff penalties, the threat of financial harm became real in Dad's mind. He had to let him go, even though it was hard to do so. I look back on it now and realize there were signs —behavior and performance—something was going on with this fellow. But we didn't have employee assistance programs back then."

"It must have been hard without the resources and knowledge we have today," I said.

"It was, Marianne. But you and I have handled a couple of doozies, haven't we?"

Kyle was wide-eyed as I recalled the story of the hostess who suddenly ran off the restaurant's floor and barricaded herself in the ladies' room. We kept extra chairs in the lounge area, and she used one to secure the door, preventing entry. One of her co-workers alerted me right away, and I called the EAP. At the same time, the store manager called the police, which was what the EAP advised, but they said to keep it as quiet as possible. Well, an ambulance arrived as did Chicago PD and the Chicago Fire Department. Everyone descended on a situation we were trying to handle discreetly because we didn't want to set her off. The fire department was ready to break the door down, but the paramedics and one of her co-workers managed to convince her to let them in. They took her out through the kitchen on a stretcher. She was covered, so people couldn't see she was restrained. Most of her co-workers thought she was physically ill. We later learned she was off her medication. She was placed on leave while she went into treatment, got her meds regulated and came back to work. Initially, we placed her in a different restaurant, but she eventually returned to her original location.

"Do you think things might have turned out differently with Bettina if Emil had counselled her earlier?" Kyle asked.

"It's hard to tell, Kyle," I responded. "All we can do is offer resources. If the employee is willing to seek or accept help for a problem, like the hostess did, then we get a great outcome. I hate to make assumptions, but I get the sense Bettina might not have been receptive to help from us. I just hope she gets help for her problem somewhere."

As I turned my attention back to Ralph, I noticed he was trying to suppress a laugh. He caught my eye and said, "Sorry, Maryanne. I was just thinking of that poor soul, Randy, a few years back who worked in purchasing. Remember the day he showed up with half his face shaved and the other half still sporting his beard and said, 'The Master made me do it?' I can still see the stunned look on his manager's face."

"Was he off his meds too?" asked Kyle.

I paused and looked up at him. "That's what we thought initially. After he said that, he started acting erratically and saying the most bizarre things. I was able to calm him down and someone else contacted the EAP to get some advice. Meantime, a staff member thought to call his father, who was listed as his emergency contact. His father got him to a doctor, and it turned out he had a brain tumor and needed surgery. As much as I wanted to help him, I realized that as HR professionals, we aren't trained to be therapists, nor are we health care professionals credentialed to diagnose disease."

"What happened to him?" asked Kyle.

"He had the surgery and went on disability for almost a year. We had a job for him once he was released, but the residual effects made it difficult for him to stick to a standard work schedule, so he declined the offer. He had a talent for drawing and started doing free-lance work as a graphic artist, giving him more control of his schedule. His wife got a job at his father's company so they would have medical insurance. He's done some work for us over the years and last I heard, he was doing okay both medically and financially."

"They weren't all good ole days," said Ralph. "Okay folks, enough reminiscing. I've got to be on a call in 15 minutes. Thanks again for a good job, Kyle."

CHAPTER 11

Slipping & Sliding

I really love my job. I really love my job. Stuck in horrible traffic on the expressway on my way to work, horns honking around me, I kept repeating this mantra while remembering my attitude about HR when I first entered the profession. *It's wonderful. What we do is so valuable for the employees and the organization.* After dealing with a crazy competitor of Kings yesterday, and now watching someone trying to cut in front of the car next to me, I'm questioning whether or not anyone really thinks anymore. Trust me, I am not a negative person who likes to wallow in self-pity but there are days...

Here's what happened yesterday. I was on a flight back to Chicago from the annual Hospitality Industry HR Conference and, as usual, the flight was totally full. Sometimes I think I am the only one who only brings two carry-on items on the flight as I noticed people struggling with bags. The poor flight attendants were doing their best to help, but no one seemed to even acknowledge them.

I settled into my window seat, plugged in my earphones, and turned on Mozart—my music of choice when I need to tune out the rest of the world. After we took off and the flight attendant offered drinks, I asked for a soda. Before I put my earphones back in, I heard the man behind me order a double Scotch. He sounded like Alex Holmes, who works for a competing restaurant chain also based in Chicago. Funny I hadn't seen him board or even noticed him in the boarding area—but, from the sound of his slurring voice, maybe he'd been in the bar and this wasn't his first drink of the afternoon. He has the reputation of being a pretty aggressive guy who works and plays hard. I considered turning around to say hello but thought better of it. While I am usually friendly to everyone, even competitors, we don't know each other that well, and I just wanted to chill. It was a curious thing, however, that since he boarded after me, he didn't say hello or acknowledge me at all. Then again, I was sitting in a window, not aisle, seat. Anyway, it wasn't my concern nor that important.

Whoever he was talking to, Alex was bemoaning his company's drop in profits at some of their restaurants in the Midwest markets and complaining about the very innovative new menu items Kings had introduced in the last quarter, almost implying we were working to either put his company out of business or buy them out. He talked about Ralph's family and how they'd been able to stay in business for so many years and wondered what our secret to success might be, hinting that maybe we were unethical. The more he drank, the louder he got, and when the flight attendant finally refused to serve him, he got very angry. I was really concerned we would be seeing an incident of air rage.

Alex's suggestions that Kings was somehow unethical were really unnerving. Ralph Napoli is a great businessman and so ethical and honest. He's taken a small chain of family restaurants and grown it by taking the time to understand our customers and our products and by always putting the customer first. There's no magic in that—just hard work. I knew I'd have to share what I was hearing from Alex with Ralph and wasn't looking forward to it. Ethics is his hot button, and Kings' reputation is everything to him and to all of us who support him.

Rethinking my earlier decision not to say hello, now Alex needed to know I heard him. So, I raised my head over the seat and turned so he could see me. He looked horror struck as he quickly realized he had shared some information that was proprietary to his company and had said some not so nice things about my company. He calmed down and was quiet for the remainder of the flight but couldn't avoid me as we deplaned. He looked at me with a sheepish expression, but not a word was exchanged.

I emailed Ralph to tell him what happened, and he called a Leadership Team meeting for first thing this morning. Ralph and Tom Edan, who is president of the competing chain Alex works for, know and respect each other. Without a doubt, Ralph would be upset that the competition was badmouthing Kings and our meeting this morning was certain to be a lively one.

Barely arriving in time for the meeting, I took my usual place next to Ralph. Our Leadership Team is so strong and we work together well—for the most part. Meetings usually start off with some casual conversation but not today. As in most organizations, we take our cues from our leader and today, Ralph was all business. As soon as everyone had coffee, he said, "Maryanne, please fill the rest of the group in on what you heard last night on the plane and before you start, let me be clear, I am taking this very seriously."

I looked around the table and all eyes were fixed on me like never before, and it wasn't a comfortable feeling. Rather than drag out the suspense, I shared what I'd overheard on the flight. Emphasis was on the lack of judgment I'd observed in Alex and his heavy drinking on the flight.

They listened carefully and asked a few questions. It didn't take long for the group to decide the best course of action would be for Ralph to call Tom Edan and fill him in on what I'd heard on the flight. We quickly moved our discussion to Alex's remarks. Had what he said meant his company might be vulnerable to a takeover and if so, should we jump on it? Ralph asked our CFO, Larry Blackstone, and his finance team to work with marketing to come up with a plan in case the opportunity existed for Kings to expand by purchasing a competing organization. Kings has been successful over the years by acquiring other chains, and this may be a golden opportunity for another win.

Once this decision was made, everyone relaxed. I took a lot of kidding about being a spy for Kings. We talked a lot about how too much alcohol can really mess up a person's judgment.

Ralph leaned back in his chair, the tension lessening in his body. "A colleague, another CEO, recently learned a very painful lesson. I'll call my friend Sam to keep his confidence. He told me he'd hired an old college roommate whom he hadn't seen in years, but who had a great resume. For a while, he did a great job in outside sales for this company, but then Sam began to notice he was taking really long lunches and when he returned to the office, he sometimes smelled like he'd been drinking."

I was thinking about how acceptable drinking at lunch was in the past. Old movies reminded us the three martini lunches were the norm. Our executives know drinking at lunch is frowned upon.

"It happened enough that other people in the office began mentioning it to Sam, so he knew he had to deal with it. But, like so many times, situations sort of resolve themselves." Ralph stopped talking and looked around the table. "Don't leave us hanging—what happened?" I said.

"One afternoon, he came back from a very long lunch, fell off his chair, and was snoring alongside his desk. Sam said that did it for him. They fired the guy on the spot."

Since this was one of those *teachable moments* HR doesn't get very often, I asked my colleagues if they thought that was the right decision. They all said yes. Then I asked a follow-up question. Did anyone think that perhaps he should have been referred to the EAP to get help before being terminated?

There was silence as I noticed my colleagues fidgeting and squirming. Finally, Larry cleared his throat and said he thought the reason managers prefer these sorts of issues resolve themselves is because they really want to avoid conflict. Heads were nodding in agreement, so I asked why they thought that way. Most of them said managers don't like to be out of control, and when you are in a conflict situation, you aren't sure of the outcome. Ralph frowned and explained that he didn't want us to be a company which ran from conflict. He wanted us to understand conflict, learn from it, and use it to innovate. I made a mental note to add conflict management skill development to our next off-site meeting and to talk to Noelle Livingston, my training and development director, about it.

This led to a good discussion about the wonderful help our EAP is to our managers, but the consensus about Sam's story was since the person was new to the organization, it didn't make sense to invest resources into someone who came with issues. I disagreed and explained I would have put him on administrative leave and referred him to the EAP. If he sought treatment and returned to work, I would have given him a second chance. I didn't think his length of service should determine whether or not he got help.

Larry isn't one to usually share stories in meetings, but he spoke up again. "This reminds me of something that happened at my last job. We had a group of executives that frequently went out for lunch together. I don't think drinking was part of the usual pattern, but it may have been because I wasn't ever invited. You all know I eat at my desk most days."

Some knowing glances were being exchanged as I thought of all the times we'd asked Larry to join us for lunch and he never did. We'd tried to entice him by telling him these lunches were work related since we either went to one of our restaurants or to a competitor to *shop the competition*, but even those arguments didn't work on him. We finally gave up asking. His stoic personality just didn't allow him to socialize on any level.

"One day the group planned to meet at their usual place," Larry was saying, "a place which was quite near our offices. For some reason they didn't drive together so one of the guys, I'll call him Noah, got there first and went to the bar to wait for the others to arrive. He waited and waited and had a couple of beers. He kept checking his phone to see if he had the time or place wrong, but no messages appeared so he just stayed and—drank for several hours. His big mistake was to go back to the office. If he'd been smart, he'd have just called a cab and gone home but no, he went back to the office. When he got to the office, he made another critical mistake. Rather than going to his office and closing the door, he went to the COO's office and demanded to know why he'd been stood up. She apologized and said she'd been called into an emergency meeting with the business development staff on a potential piece of new business. She said they should have called or texted him to let him know they weren't coming but things were moving quickly, and it just slipped her mind."

We were all picturing this scene while Larry continued his story. "As she was apologizing, Noah jumped up onto her desk, scattering papers and empty coffee cups all over the place, and just sat down—right in the middle of her desk. The COO grabbed her phone and called the facilities manager to come help her. It was a miracle they got him out to the street and into a cab without seeing anyone else from the office."

"Bet Noah never came back to work. He had to be mortified at what he'd done in his manager's office," I said.

Larry gave me a slight smile, which surprised me. He's not one to show emotion. "Yes, I agree that if it had been me, I'd have left the state without even getting my final paycheck, but Noah was a very valuable employee. He had a good relationship with a very difficult supplier, so we didn't want to fire him until we could evaluate what his firing would do to our business. So, we did what Maryanne mentioned a moment ago—we called our EAP and got help for him. The good news was it bought us the time we needed to pick his brain, but the bad news was he didn't stay sober for very long and very soon thereafter was terminated for poor performance."

As people mulled over the implications of Larry's story, I thought about how pragmatic he is but then, I guess it's a good trait for a CFO. Someday I hope Larry surprises me by showing some human compassion—even some recognition of the people side of the business. I can dream, can't I?

Brian Chang, our young and totally engaged CTO, usually has the best stories. "How about this? My last company did a lot of sales incentive trips as rewards for our top performers, and the executive team was always included so we could use it as a team building event. This particular trip was a five-day cruise, and we each were invited to bring our significant other. Needless to say, there was a lot of drinking—especially on the one day we spent on the ship sailing to the private island. Late in the afternoon when everyone was around the pool sipping those rum drinks that sneak up on you, one of the sales managers—who wasn't beloved by his team—went down the waterslide and ripped out the back of his bathing suit. He was so blitzed, he didn't realize what had happened. He walked around the pool for at least a half hour, and no one told him his behind was totally exposed. Finally, someone took pity on him and let him know his butt was hanging out, so he put a towel around himself and paraded around the pool. Others who were equally buzzed, decided to make a drinking game of it and chased him around the pool—whenever anyone could pick up the towel and expose the butt, everyone took a drink."

"Brian, why didn't you tell him?" I said.

"Because Susie and I had booked a couples massage on the ship that afternoon and didn't hear about it until dinner. If I'd been there, I would have spoken up. But apparently everyone was so drunk, they just enjoyed the show. Since no one really liked him, it made it even juicier."

Frowning, Ralph looked at Brian. "Did your company change its incentive trips after that incident? I know I would have."

"No, which is one of the reasons I left. I couldn't deal with the infantile behavior that was reinforced by the leadership. I admire how we do things here at Kings. We have a good time at company events, but we don't have open bars or put people in situations where they are tempted to misbehave."

I left the meeting and called the HR team together for a quick update. I didn't tell them about my experience on the plane but asked them to be thinking about our holiday parties. How we could send the message to our employees that misbehavior at a company function can have serious implications for your future employment? This was also a moment to reinforce that one of HR's roles is to model good behavior at work. I knew my team really well, but it never hurts to remind them we're in the spotlight and their behavior is monitored by the rest of the organization.

CHAPTER 12

Not So Social Media

I could hear the rain pounding against the window in my office, but it was music compared to the combative voice on the other end of the phone. The caller was relentless, barely giving me an opportunity to respond. Finally, she paused, and I took advantage of it.

"If you'll give me a moment to speak," I said, "I can clarify a few things. I can understand that this appears to be a distressing situation, but Kings doesn't discuss employee issues with outsiders. If I can get some facts from you, I'll be able to look into the situation—but no, I won't, I can't, call you back and tell you the outcome."

Meanwhile, I looked up and saw my assistant Ryan standing in the doorway frantically trying to get my attention, but I waived him away. Not taking the cue, he walked over to the whiteboard and scribbled *Ralph wants to see you, NOW.* I cradled the phone on my shoulder almost dropping it as I grabbed a piece of paper and pen and wrote, *Tell him I've got a hot one on the line—I'll be there ASAP.*

He scribbled the words *Death Threat* on the white board. I pointed to the phone, shook my head, and mouthed the words *I know.*

As the caller started in again, I interrupted her. "Ma'am, we can't share information about our employees with you. *That's* the bottom line. I appreciate your bringing this situation to my attention. We'll look into it. *Now,* I have to end this conversation."

"I will call back. You haven't heard the last of me," she retorted.

As I hung up the phone, my hands were shaking, but it didn't stop me from slamming my fist on the desk. *I shouldn't let this get to me, but she was so nasty,* I thought. *And something didn't sound right.* Ryan was back in the doorway. "Right. Ralph. On my way," I said jumping up and brushing past him.

I was no sooner at Ralph's office door when I heard Bob Zimmerman, our COO, saying, "Death threats? Hell, Ralph, this sounds serious."

I burst in. "Ralph, is this a complaint about a Facebook post made by Wyatt Driscoll? I got a similar call."

"When?" Ralph almost barked at me.

"Just got off it. That's why I wasn't here sooner."

"Folks, we've got to do something, and fast. We need to get Valerie London in here. We need our General Counsel involved in this."

"She's on vacation, Ralph," said Bob. "I know this is upsetting, but let's all take a deep breath and figure out exactly what we know. Ralph, why don't you tell Maryanne what you told me about the call you took?"

Ralph motioned for me to sit down. "When this guy got on the line, he sounded very amicable—said he enjoyed eating at Kings' restaurants and had great respect for us. That's why he thought I should know we had an employee who posed a threat to the community. He said we needed to report Wyatt to the police and fire him. When I asked him why, he said he was posting death threats against Kaplan, that joker who's running for an alderman position on the city council."

"Did he tell you what Wyatt said in his posts?" Bob asked.

"Something about guns and shooting up all the candidates in Kaplan's party. I asked him his name and how he happened to come by this information—that's when he exploded, screaming we had an employee who was violent, and we'd better do something about it. I thanked him for bringing this to our attention but told him I'd manage my own company's employees. Look, I don't get all this social media stuff. And who is this Wyatt Driscoll?"

Bob turned to me and said, "Your turn, Maryanne."

"Ralph, Wyatt works in marketing, in Tim Davidson's group. My call wasn't much different, except the woman I spoke with didn't start off very friendly. She sounded like one of those marketing calls where they just start talking and don't let you get a word in. She said she was calling on behalf of Kaplan and the party, claiming Wyatt was advocating violence against all the members of the party. She even implied he was calling for some type of a shoot-out. Whenever I tried to get more information, she just kept shouting at me. The only thing I could understand was something about Facebook. She asked me pointedly what I intended to do about it. That was about the time Ryan came in to alert me about your call, Ralph."

Bob was maintaining a cool head about this situation, which was a relief. We've worked together for nearly four years since he was hired as our first Chief Operating Office, and he's always been a steady presence. I couldn't explain why I was letting this caller get under my skin, but I was really upset—by the call and the situation. As I turned to look at him, I realized he was talking.

"We all know it's been a contentious political season in Chicago, like that's anything new. Between the prickly remarks during the recent debates and the comments on social media, things are getting rather ugly. Maryanne, do you think we can pull up Wyatt's Facebook profile?"

I was already doing so on my phone. Apparently, in response to a string of Facebook posts and comments, Wyatt wrote that *someone needs to put these suffering bastards out of their misery* followed by a string of gun emoji. It was an obvious reference to several candidates from one party. This apparently struck a nerve with members of those candidates' party, and they concluded the remark represented death threats and Wyatt had violent tendencies. Through his Facebook profile, they identified Kings as his employer and decided—either independently or together—to take the action they did this morning.

"Maryanne, would you agree we don't have enough information to act on just yet?"

"Absolutely, Bob. We can't determine if this is a veiled threat of violence or an example of monumental bad judgment, as Valerie would say. We don't know if he did this during work hours, if he used a Kings computer to do this, or if he somehow implicated Kings other than listing us as his employer. We don't even know if he did it. His account could have been hacked. Stuff like that happens all the time."

"How much do we know about this employee?" asked Ralph. "And assuming this isn't the so-called death threat, doesn't he have a first amendment right to say whatever stupid-ass thing he wants to say? Maryanne, can you get your husband Jack on the phone?"

Maintaining a calm composure, Bob turned and looked first in my direction, then directly at our boss. "Ralph, let's prioritize our actions before we start placing calls to lawyers. And Maryanne, doesn't Valerie prefer to use a law firm other than your husband's—conflict of interest and all that?"

We decided we first needed to talk with Wyatt's manager, and Bob said he and I could do that. As I could recall, there'd never been any negative issues or feedback about him, but I'd check his file to be sure. We agreed if any additional calls came in, including from this morning's callers, Ralph and I would refer them to Bob, so they'd all be channeled to the same person. Bob would work with me and outside counsel on an appropriate response. After we'd talked with Wyatt's manager, Bob and I would place a call to outside counsel. We'd reconvene this afternoon in Ralph's office after Bob and I had more information.

As we left Ralph's office, Bob turned and said, "This really has you rattled, Maryanne. I've never seen you this distressed."

"I know. It's just this damn social media is like dealing with the Wild West sometimes. And not only at work, but do you know what it's like having two teenage daughters in this day and age?"

"I can certainly sympathize," he said as we walked into his office. He went right to his desk, picked up the phone and called Wyatt's manager, Dale, requesting he come up right away. While we were waiting, I called Kyle and asked him to pull Wyatt's file and check to see if there were any negative write ups or performance reviews, and to lock the file in my office when he was done. I'd explain later.

When Dale came to the door, he was surprised to see me there as well. "Please. Come in, Dale, take a seat and relax. Don't let Maryanne frighten you. Just because HR's here doesn't mean you're in trouble," Bob said. It was the first time I'd smiled since this mess started earlier.

Dale was surprised when we told him about the calls and allegations regarding Wyatt. "This is not like him. He's a good employee—gets along with everyone—well respected by me and his co-workers. He's *very* easy going and mild mannered." Dale assured us Wyatt never exhibited any type of unusual behavior, either in the office or at after-hours social events. "He never discusses politics. This just doesn't sound like something he'd do—especially not at work."

We hadn't established if a work computer was used, and Bob was hinting we should get IT involved. I wanted to wait until we talked with the attorneys. I asked Dale to keep this quiet and not discuss it with anyone except Bob or me until we had more information. At this point, no one was accusing Wyatt of any wrongdoing at work. And if there was some underlying problem, we weren't aware of, we certainly didn't want to set him off.

After Dale left, Bob walked to his computer to look up the phone number for Gabe Krantz, the outside employment attorney Valerie uses. While he was doing that, I called Kyle. No, there was nothing in Wyatt's file out of the ordinary. All good performance reviews. I hung up, handed the phone to Bob so he could call the attorney.

When Gabe came on the line, Bob put him on speaker and related the events of the morning. I told Gabe in detail about my conversation with the woman. Then I told him we were looking for some general guidance before we proceeded. I asked about having IT investigate if he used a company computer—they routinely did check for inappropriate computer use. His advice was it wouldn't hurt, but it all depended on how much suspicion we wanted to raise. The more straightforward approach might be to just confront Wyatt and ask him.

When Bob brought up Ralph's point about freedom of speech, Gabe said it's only applicable when the U.S. Government says you can't express your views, not your employer. Surprisingly, Gabe told us people get fired all the time for social media postings. I wondered why I never heard this from Jack.

"If the ultimate decision is to fire Wyatt, he couldn't claim Kings violated his constitutional freedom," Gabe advised.

"We're not at the point of making a decision just yet, Gabe," I said.

"Maryanne, has this employee ever shown a propensity for violence?" Gabe asked. I described how Dale portrayed him and explained there was nothing in his employment history with us to suggest it.

"That's good. If he did have such a propensity, and then acted out in the workplace, and it turned out this post was, in fact, a threat, the company wouldn't have a defense. Just something to think about if you decide not to fire him. Take some steps to mitigate any possible future harm. In fact, Maryanne, you may want to strengthen your social media policy so employees know what they can and can't do."

"Thanks, Gabe. You've given us some good guidance. We'll let you know if we need anything else."

Bob disconnected the call and turned to me. "I can quietly ask Brian Chang in IT if there's been any unusual computer usage, especially in Dale's department." He glanced at his watch—it was almost noon—and suggested bringing something in and discussing next steps over lunch. Where had the morning gone?

Once we finished eating and cleared lunch away, I checked in with my staff who must have thought I was missing in action by now. Bob checked with Brian, but there'd been nothing alarming or unusual in computer usage during the past month. We called Dale and asked him if he and Wyatt could come to Bob's office for a meeting. I cautioned Dale not to give any details—to let Bob and I take the lead in the meeting.

True to Dale's description, Wyatt was very polite and easy-going. He didn't appear nervous being called into a meeting with the COO and CHRO. I began by explaining two calls had come that morning—one to me and one to Ralph—and both callers, from outside the company, made some serious allegations about him. I stressed we were here to get to the facts, first-hand from him, and then told him the allegations. Before, I could explain anything further, his demeanor changed. His eyes were welling up, and I thought he was about to burst into tears. But he didn't.

He shot up in the chair and in a sharp voice said, "If you're going to fire me over this, go ahead. But I think I've got rights—freedom to speak—and you can't dictate what I do on my own time. I want to talk to a lawyer."

Dale's face went white. I'm sure he was thinking, I just vouched for Wyatt. Where is this outburst coming from?

Bob shrugged, nodding his head in Wyatt's direction, before saying, "Take a deep breath. We're not accusing you of anything, Wyatt, but we do need to know if you posted that comment on Facebook or if your account was hacked. The company became involved because you listed Kings in your Facebook profile as your employer. We're just trying to sort this all out."

I leaned forward in my chair. "Wyatt, we have no reason to believe that you used a work computer, nor do we have any interest in monitoring all of our employees' activities all the time. Put yourself in our shoes for just a minute. Mr. Napoli and I were thrown by those calls today and none of us appreciated the allegations the callers were making without knowing all the facts. Reality is, we don't know if this is the last we'll hear from these people, and we want to get ahead of it."

Wyatt slumped back into the chair. "I'm so sorry. I didn't...I mean I never intended to embarrass Kings—this company has been great to work for." His voice was shaking. "Watching that debate the other night got me so upset, and I'd had a few beers, and that one idiot running for alderman in my ward just kept saying such stupid things—it just set me off. My buddy saw that Twitter was rampant with comments and started tweeting. Then I responded to a string of posts on Facebook. It wasn't meant as a threat."

"Look, Wyatt," I said, "this has been upsetting for all of us and a very unfortunate occurrence. I can certainly understand someone pushing your buttons and reacting—it's human. That woman I spoke with this morning certainly pushed a few of mine. This election season has been pretty nasty and, unfortunately, it's bringing out the worst in people."

I thought I saw Wyatt's eyes watering as he turned to look at Dale. "I never meant to...I mean I never thought it would come to this. If it'll help, I'll resign."

Dale looked at me, wide eyed, swallowed and started to say something to Wyatt, but Bob interjected. "We're not asking for your resignation, Wyatt. As Maryanne said, we just needed to get to the bottom of this."

It sounded like air going out of a balloon as Wyatt and Dale breathed a collective sigh of relief. I turned to Wyatt and said, "I need to make a very strong suggestion though. Since the nature of your Facebook comments were arguably interpreted as possible threats, please consider contacting our EAP and meeting with a counselor for at least a few sessions. Talk things through with a professional."

He seemed hesitant for a moment, and I wasn't sure if he was resisting my suggestion. Dale caught his eye and nodded which I saw as a sign of agreement with me. His head was hanging down as he said, almost in a whisper, "I'll do that Maryanne." Then he looked up and said to Bob and me, "And I'll change my Facebook profile and start using an alias. Thanks so much for not firing me."

Once they left, Bob turned to me. "Before we brief Ralph, what did you think about Gabe's suggestion about our social media policy?"

"You know, my husband, Jack, and I have this discussion all the time. Lawyers seem to think policies are the answer to everything, but all the policies in the world aren't going to change behavior. We can't be in the business of policing everything our employees do—and how would we enforce such a policy? What we can do is issue an advisory to all our employees stating while we don't want to monitor their personal activity on line or elsewhere, it's important to recognize that listing your employer in a social media profile can come back and tarnish the company. So, think carefully about what you post on different social media platforms—how it represents you and the company. Recognize you have a personal brand you may portray on Facebook, a professional brand you may project on LinkedIn—but be cautious of how your brands may reflect on the company's brand and values."

"That's excellent, Maryanne. And we should probably suggest to Ralph that our public relations team be put on notice to draft something just in case either of these yahoos decide to make this public. It's no secret how important the company's reputation is to Ralph."

I nodded in agreement as Bob picked up the phone to call Ralph, who summoned us to his office right away. He was relieved to hear the situation was under control and asked Bob to take the lead with PR.

The rest of the afternoon flew by. Jack was picking me up at 5:30 sharp tonight so we could get to a function at the girls' school. As soon as I slid into the front seat, he greeted me with a big smile. "How was your day?" he asked. I let out a sigh and proceeded to recount the day's events, leaving out Gabe's advice about our social media policy.

"Hopefully, this will be the end of it. Patti Griffith, one of our associates, encountered a peculiar situation recently. An employee of one of our clients claimed, among other things, that co-workers are spying on him through social media. He told his manager he overheard people in the hallway making references to a little penis and is convinced they are referring to a picture he took of himself and sent to his ex-girlfriend. He thinks they got a copy of it somehow and are spreading it around cyberspace using company devices to do so, although he didn't have any proof."

I think I missed some of what Jack was telling me. I was making a mental note that I had to have a serious talk with our girls about the perils associated with irresponsible use of social platforms.

Then I heard Jack saying, "Patti was urging them to rewrite their policy—she'd even begun drafting something—but that idea was vetoed."

Undoubtedly it was, I thought, but didn't say it. Jack was still talking.

"Most companies have policies about the proper use of their internal networks. It's good to issue an advisory from time to time reminding employees about the proper use of not only company devices, but the company's systems that support those devices. And regardless of who owns the device, if it's used to access the Internet through the corporate network, it could be a violation of policy, especially if they access unauthorized sites. Bottom line, companies have the right to control and monitor what happens on their systems."

"What happened with the guy? Were people spying on him?"

"Doubtful," said Jack. His ex didn't work for the company and there was no evidence he used the company network to send the photo."

"Social media," I sighed. "Stephanie told us an interesting story about the college the last time our networking group met."

"Are you going to share?" asked Jack.

Apparently, a young man had been hired to work in the communications department—web design, social media responsibilities. He did really good work and was a reliable employee, but he had other aspirations. His dream was to be a rapper, and he was filming rap videos during his lunch breaks. The filming did not seem to be disruptive to anyone. No one was aware he was doing this until his videos began to pop up on YouTube when you did a search for the college. It seems he used the campus as a backdrop with signs and prominent buildings visible.

"So, what did they do? Was there anything inherently egregious about the videos?"

"Oh, Jack, stop talking like a lawyer all the time," I teased. "No, there was nothing inappropriate about the content of the videos, but rap videos weren't exactly the image the college wanted to depict. They acknowledged his creativity but explained he shouldn't be using the workplace for his hobby nor to advance aspirations which weren't job related. Just like Wyatt, he was very remorseful. He quickly offered to take the videos down—which he did. Because of his attitude, they just documented the verbal counseling and didn't give him a written reprimand. He wrote a letter of apology to the dean, too. Because of his positive actions and creative talents, his manager gave him more challenging assignments."

As we pulled into the parking lot of the girl's school, Jack turned to me and said, "Sounds like the lesson from Stephanie's story is as different generations come together, all of us have to gain some awareness of each other's perspective."

Yes, we are in a brave, new world, I thought.

CHAPTER 13

Silence is Golden

David Morgan's laugh was infectious. I could hear him from across the hall as I was signing for the food for tonight's networking meeting at my office. As everyone was settling in, Linda Goodman was talking about a new comedy she and her wife, Millie, had seen at the movies this past weekend.

Jason Edison was sitting back in his chair with a wry smile. "Secrets, cheating spouses, corporate lies, and leaks. Sounds like this movie had it all, a fiasco that could happen anywhere. And I don't think I'd be breaching any confidentiality if I shared an incident which happened last week at my firm." That got everyone's attention.

"One of our consultants was doing a workplace investigation for a law firm. The client thought it would be less intimidating if someone other than an attorney did the interviews. A man accused a male VP of creating a hostile environment for women."

"How noble," said Linda, her blue eyes flashing. "Especially these days."

"Don't praise him so quickly," Jason responded as he continued. "Our consultant spoke with a number of people, men and women, but there was no evidence of any type of volatile or offensive behavior toward women like he intimated—sexually suggestive language, sexual, lewd or derogatory remarks about specific women in the office, or sexual jokes. There were recollections of crude language made among some of the guys behind closed doors, but no remarks targeting any specific women or women in general."

Jason paused to take a bite of his snack. "After the interviews were concluded, our consultant briefed the attorney and the client about her findings. During the call, the client, who was the COO, identified one more person who may have observed a particular something—a director, who worked closely with both the VP and the complainant. Everyone agreed the consultant should speak with the director via phone. The attorney gave very explicit instructions to the COO: 'Tell the director to expect a call from a consultant who's looking into a situation at the company. Don't discuss anything specific with him. Don't describe the nature of the allegations. We don't want to tip our hand.' The lawyer was crystal clear."

David's mouth fell open in feigned surprise as he looked directly at me. "Have you ever known a lawyer not to be crystal clear?"

Laughing, I raised my hand and swatted as it to wave his comment away, then turned to Jason. "Continue, please."

"During the phone call, the consultant asked the director: Did you ever hear the VP make derogatory comments about women? Make lewd remarks or comments? Did you ever hear the VP say anything in a public setting that would make anyone, male or female, uncomfortable? Did he ever make inappropriate comments in an open meeting? His response was no to all these questions—adding the VP knew his audience."

Fingering her reading glasses in her left hand, Stephanie Packard slowly said, "Soooo, why all the fuss? Where's the drama?"

"Seems that the director admitted the VP would occasionally say things in private—things the director didn't find offensive. When queried further, he said the VP might say 'she's a hot one' or 'look at those great legs' about random women who might be passing by on the street, but it was locker room talk—just guys in the room bonding—nothing that was a hostile work environment."

"Curious choice of words," I said

"Exactly," said Jason, "and this is where it gets interesting. The director went on to explain he was shocked when he heard about the allegations and repeated verbatim most of the comments that were alleged to have been made. It was clear to the consultant that the COO had disclosed specific details about the situation to him contrary to the attorney's instruction."

"Speaking of confidentiality, how did you happen to hear about this, Jason?" someone asked.

"I was passing the room where our consultant was making this call when I heard her slam the phone down and drop the *F-bomb*. Very out of character for her. So, I stepped into the room, closed the door, and asked her what was going on. We'd both been briefed about the situation by the law firm, so she confided in me. She needed to vent about how the COO totally blew the objectivity of this interview with the director because now the director was telling her what he thought his boss wanted to hear—not his unfiltered observations. And if he knew all of this, who else might have been told? She was so upset and afraid the attorney was going to go ballistic and blame her."

Everyone turned in my direction. "What? Just because I'm married to an attorney, doesn't mean I know what happened next," I laughed. "But I can venture a guess. The attorney probably had a follow up discussion with the client—one of those calls with the lawyers most managers dread because they get a good tongue lashing."

Jason nodded in agreement. "You realize being a consultant and outside the organization where all this took place, I'll never know for sure how the situation was resolved. But I know these lawyers well enough to offer my opinion. Since the integrity of the entire process and investigation could be called into question, they are probably recommending their client offer some sort of monetary settlement before the claim goes further. It's really a shame since the investigation hadn't uncovered any evidence of volatile behavior, unless, of course, the director who blew it knew something he wasn't telling."

"Uh, correct me if I'm wrong, Jason," I interjected, "didn't you say the individual—the client's representative—was the COO?" Jason shook his head yes.

"Why *do* people feel compelled to reveal all the dirty details?" Linda said calmly but looking like she wanted to scream.

"Because they are dirty details, and they feel empowered knowing them," Stephanie said, her eyes twinkling as she went on to tell about someone being fired for sexual harassment and the CFO wanting to know all the details from HR—what did the individual do, what did he say? He was very upset HR wouldn't tell him everything, much less anything, insisting that because the HR manager reported to *him*, locally anyway, he had the right to know *everything*.

"Was he upset she didn't confer with him about the firing?" asked Linda.

"Noooo," said Stephanie. "He could have cared less. He knew she talked to HR and legal at the corporate headquarters. He wanted to stay as far away from 'all the people stuff,' as he put it, as he could. He just wanted to hear what he thought would be sordid details. The HR manager gave him a dose of reality by asking him how he'd feel if HR talked to other employees about him and his behavior. He didn't like that, but he got the point."

As she looked up from doodling in her notepad, Linda shook her head. "Some people just don't have enough of a life. They've gotta get in the middle of everyone else's. I get that it's human nature to be curious when the rumor mill is buzzing. But we've been talking about people in responsible positions. I know we're very sensitive to issues of confidentiality in HR, but you think COOs or CFOs would have the same sensitivity and more sense than to ask about confidential information or worse, offer up details like Jason's client did. Can you imagine how a CFO would react if you asked for or spread confidential financial information?"

"Come to think of it..." I paused for a moment trying to remember all the details. "A staff member talked about the head of communications where she once worked. Quite a character. Always dropping names—drinks with so-and-so, at a party with this one—and had dozens of framed pictures of celebrities in his office. It was always all about him—who he knew, how important he was. Always trying to find out what was going on in business and social circles. Always trying to obtain an invitation to any event where he thought he should be seen. Well, over lunch one day with a reporter—they *supposedly* talked off the record—he told the reporter about a business deal the company was working on—something highly confidential."

Reaching over and grabbing my arm, Ellen Cooper, who never missed a detail, said, "Wait, Maryanne. Didn't you say he was in communications?"

"I sure did," I said. "Believe he was the communications director who set the guidelines about who could speak on behalf of the company. But I understand he often wasn't very clear when he was trying to impress people. He probably made a casual remark without indicating it was off-the-record. The reporter, to his credit, called the CEO to confirm and agreed to suppress the story in return for an exclusive interview if the deal went through. The CEO fired the director on the spot for leaking confidential information to the press."

Jason's brows were drawn together. "I'm sure the lawyers weren't happy, and we all know it's not a good idea to terminate that quickly. Sounds like it was a knee-jerk reaction. It could have been risky, unless, of course, the information was very damaging—something like insider trading."

"I don't know what the nature of the information was, other than the situation was very sensitive, I said. "The CEO was adamant. What's wrong with people? Don't these executives know the rules apply to them?"

"Oh, you know they think the rules they make apply to everyone else but them," quipped Linda. "And now with social media, their blabbing goes viral. How would any of you handled this situation I recently heard from a client? Several months ago, someone on a due diligence team posted on his Facebook page about a big contract the company won before it was announced. Not only had the company not announced it, the contract hadn't been signed yet."

"Oh, just fire him and be done with it," chuckled the ever-impartial Stephanie, "Do you know what they did, Linda? And how did you come to hear this confidential tidbit?"

"I was working with the client on staffing some key positions on the new contract, and she told me because it had raised concerns about confidentiality. Apparently, the individual who disclosed the information was hoping to be promoted into one of these key positions and probably would have but for his indiscretion."

Linda paused and looked around the table. "Naturally, she couldn't tell me what action they took. If he wasn't fired, I'd be tempted to significantly decrease any compensation he'd receive for his involvement in this deal. But with this talk about the media relations folks, it's a good opportunity to remind employees about social media and their role in communication. The guidelines about who can speak to the media go beyond just talking to reporters. They apply to anything you say about the company or anything you post on a social media platform. It's not just a message of zip your lips. Communication is more than just talking."

Stephanie picked up her bottle of water and realized it was empty. "Here, let me get another for you, Stephanie," said David who was closer to the drinks set out on the credenza behind him.

Twisting off the cap, Stephanie turned to look at Jason. "You mentioned insider trading. Have you, or any of you, had any experience with that issue?"

All heads around the table were shaking from left to right, with a few eyes glancing upward indicating relief this was one issue no one had encountered. Then I remembered something. "Most of you know my husband Jack comes from a family of lawyers. When he was in law school, his uncle in New York was trying to entice him to move there when he graduated—regaling Jack with stories of the excitement he could experience. His uncle's firm did a lot of mergers and acquisitions in the late 1980s. Since confidentiality was a big issue, all employees had to sign an annual statement saying they wouldn't discuss work-related issues with anyone outside the office—including family. It seems after work one night in a midtown bar, two guys got to talking about a deal involving two publicly traded companies. It took less than 24 hours for word to get back to the firm, and possibly the SEC. The two were escorted out of the building by the police in handcuffs, quickly terminated, and likely prosecuted, though Jack's uncle never said so. Pretty dramatic, and I'm sure it sent a powerful message and reminder to all the employees about confidentiality—no inter-office memos required."

"Interoffice memos. Anyone remember those?" laughed Jason. "We can only speculate those two characters not only discussed confidential information in public, but also discussed acting on information they had. Insider trading violations are an enforcement priority for the SEC. But from an HR standpoint, the 80s were a different time. The culture was quick to terminate employees, or so I've heard from older colleagues. It was less risky then—people were less litigious. I'm sure the managing partner took care of all the messy details."

David's mood had changed dramatically since the beginning of the meeting. He was sitting across from me, and I couldn't help but notice the long sigh he breathed before shaking his head and saying, "I feel like Pandora trying to figure out what to do with what she found in that box. I've got a dilemma I'd like to run by everyone."

All eyes turned to him. His tech company had acquired a smaller firm about eighteen months ago, with an office in Denver which they closed. Most of the staff was relocated to Chicago. At the time of the acquisition, a lawsuit was pending, and one of the relocated staff members had to fly to Denver to testify. He was sitting in a hotel lobby bar one night, you know one of those large, open ones with couches, tables, and workstations. He was drinking and chatting things up with the person next to him who was somewhat of a braggart, like the communications director we spoke of earlier.

"Too much to drink, too much ego, too great a desire to impress this stranger by sharing details, whatever his motivation, he proceeded to talk about his trip and details of the lawsuit. Who knows exactly what he said, but it caught the attention of an attorney on the other side of the case who was sitting nearby. Next morning that attorney called our outside law firm, who called our corporate legal office, who wanted him fired. But his management loves him, great employee, valuable employee, you know the script. They're willing to overlook this as a small indiscretion."

Heads were shaking back and forth again, this time in sympathy with David's predicament when Jason raised up his hand. "Hold on. Now the attorneys *want* him fired right away? No investigation?"

"Well, the rules don't apply when they're involved," said Ellen. "Un-Effing-Believable and I'm pretty sure that's a legal term. I've heard lawyers use it. Any chance this is going to damage your company's position on the case?"

"Too soon to tell that, and once I calmed in-house counsel down, I convinced him things might not be as bad as everyone thought. We don't know exactly what details he might have disclosed nor what this other attorney actually heard. Still, we've got to do something. Yes, our workplace behavior policy covers confidentiality, and our ethics program also covers it. But these folks think in terms of proprietary data or products and not necessarily people issues. It all goes back to curiosity about the dirty details. I want to send a strong message that not only is gossiping about other people's behavior not tolerated but disclosing facts in a lawsuit could cost the company money, just like discussing facts about our proprietary technology."

While David was talking, Stephanie appeared to be staring off into space. "David, could you suspend him for a week without pay? That would hurt him monetarily and his absence could send a message to his co-workers."

"In our environment, it probably wouldn't work, and our policy isn't that explicit. See, these techies are so wired into work, he'd still be in touch with everyone. And I don't want to come right out and tell everyone what he did. I'm not looking to make an example of him. Good thought, Stephanie, but I doubt it would do much good."

Tapping her forefinger on the table, Ellen's attention was focused on David. "It looks like you have two points to make here, David. First, this guy's got to understand there are consequences to what he did, and you want to make the consequences effective and fitting for the situation, right? Second, you have to make it clear to him, to the management staff, to everyone, that confidentiality isn't limited just to certain topics."

A slow smile came across David's face. "You're exactly right, Ellen. Whatever action I suggest taking has to be fitting and effective. And Linda, you said something earlier about decreasing compensation. That gives me an idea. This guy is eligible for a bonus. I could suggest we either withhold it or decrease its amount because of this. That should get his attention—point out his actions could have financial consequences for the company. He has to share the pain as well as the success. I'll just have to convince his management team."

Jason glanced at his watch. "Well another good evening, my friends, but I'm afraid I've got to head out. I know what I'll take away from tonight's discussion. There were some good examples and ideas here which can form the basis of case studies for our ethics training this year. I'm on the committee to work on it, and I've hit the mother lode tonight. I'll let you all know how it progresses."

"That would be great," said David. "That might be the answer to the second part of my dilemma—educating people about ethics, confidentiality, and consequences. But one step at a time."

With that everyone stood up to leave. I waved off offers to help clean up, bid everyone goodbye as I took the food which was left into the kitchen. The janitorial crew would appreciate it. I wish all business meetings could be as productive as the ones I have with my networking group.

CHAPTER 14

That Bitch!

There was a loud knock on my door before it flew open and my assistant Ryan rushed in. "Sorry for the interruption, but Larry Blackstone wants you to come up to his office right away. He says it's urgent."

I looked up at Gloria Lincoln. We were going over the results from the latest benefits survey for Chicagoland. I knew Larry, our CFO, wouldn't be thrilled to hear about rising health care and other benefit costs.

About to protest, thinking Larry probably didn't request my presence but demanded it, Gloria waved her hand, gesturing me to go. "We've got to pick our battles with him carefully, Maryanne." As the oldest member of my staff, Gloria, Director of Employee Benefits, often serves as my anchor and sounding board, especially when things get tough.

"Okay. But leave the report here on the table. Let's plan to get back to it as soon as I return." Gloria looked up and just sighed. I sensed she was thinking we wouldn't be finishing this discussion anytime soon.

"Thank you, Ryan. Let Larry know I'll be there in just a few minutes." Gloria and I both rose from the table, and I followed her out of my office closing the door behind me. I decided to take the stairs up to the sixth floor. It will give me a chance to prepare for whatever Larry is planning to throw at me this time.

Larry and I have the classic conflict between HR and finance. He thinks I *only* see the people side—the soft side, as he says—of business. I think he *only* sees the number side of business. As I entered the stairwell, I couldn't help but think what else I could do to bridge our differences. He often acts like a bully in management meetings, but he and Ralph have worked together for many years, and Ralph has a tendency to agree with his opinions in many discussions. When I recommended team coaching for our Leadership Team, Ralph resisted, and I'm sure it was because Larry has persuaded him to do so. Larry fails to see its value.

As I approached his office, Larry's assistant pointed to the conference room. I could tell from her expression there was no time for exchanging pleasantries and that he *was not* in a good mood.

Larry was pacing across the back of the room when I entered. At first, he wasn't aware I was there. When he finally saw me, he bellowed: "Look, Maryanne, we've got a big problem in Nashville. And I don't think any amount of coaching is going to save Kenesha." My inner voice was telling me *soften your face, relax your shoulders, soften your voice*.

"Larry, can you please tell me what's going on," I said taking a seat at the conference room table. "And please join me and sit." He pulled out a chair at the head of the table—always has to be the one in control—and reluctantly sat down.

"We've discovered credit card fraud in the Nashville region."

"In one of the restaurants? By a customer?"

"No, among the staff," he shot back.

Kings had recently expanded into Nashville by buying a regional chain there. Kenesha Washington was selected to be the District Manager because she had been very successful as a district manager in Indianapolis. She's hard-working and dedicated but under a lot of pressure to show results in Nashville quickly. Ralph isn't known for his patience when it comes to results. There is a lot of remodeling going on which is not helping her get the sales up. I recognized early she'd enjoyed success in the past, but this new area involved integrating employees from the former chain into the Kings' culture—a new challenge for her. So I fought to get her an executive coach to assure her success.

He leaned toward me and slapped his hand against the table. "You do understand, don't you, Maryanne, that Ralph has been breathing down my neck over this new region. He wants it to be profitable and wants it fast."

I could feel my shoulders tensing. "I know that Larry, but let's talk about this fraud issue. And how does it relate to profitability?" My tone had hardened, and I knew I needed to get this conversation focused. Listening to Larry pontificate about unrelated matters wasn't going to solve the problem. "Tell me specifically what is going on in Nashville involving credit card fraud."

Larry took a deep breath, crossed his arms, and leaned back in the chair. "A number of irregular charges on the company credit card for a staff member were reported to us. Even though the employee gets the monthly statement and is responsible for paying it, we get copies and are alerted if there is any unusual activity—such as, charges for large consumer items not associated with normal business activity."

"I'm not following," I said. "Are you sure the charges aren't associated with the remodeling that's going on?"

"That's not exactly it." Larry swiveled his chair around and was looking out the window. The gray sky and the clouds were signaling a storm. I had a feeling it was nothing compared to the one brewing in here. "It seems there were a number of charges for entertainment establishments."

"Can you be more specific, Larry?"

"There was one for Hooters, which occurred the evening after a scheduled staff meeting of all of the restaurant managers and..." his voice trailing off.

"Surely you're not implying Kenesha took her staff..."

Larry turned and shifted his gaze back to me. "No Maryanne, and let me finish, there's more. Around the same time there were a number of charges at a local package store. But the most disturbing charge was made at Pure Gold Crazy Horse, a gentleman's club in Nashville. It was for over $2,000. There was also a cash advance for about $400."

"Were these charges all made by the same person?"

"Yes, they were all made by Pete Jackson."

It took every fiber of my being to not enact the scene playing out in my head. Pete Jackson had been the General Manager of the restaurant chain we purchased in Nashville. He and Larry had hit it off during the negotiation process. Larry got the idea since Pete knew the marketplace and the staff, we should place him on a retainer agreement as Assistant District Manager reporting directly to Kenesha but with a dotted line to Judy Marshall, the VP of Food & Beverage, at least for the transition period. All of the district managers reported to her. This decision to retain Pete as Assistant DM ran counter to our business model, and both Judy and I were opposed to it. Somehow Larry had convinced Ralph it was a good idea which perplexed us all since it would be a drain on profits. Were either of them looking at the numbers?

I wanted to scream at Larry. *It was your idea to keep him on. What were you thinking?* But reason prevailed. I took a deep breath before I asked the next questions. "Have all the charges been paid to the credit card company? Did he try to expense any of these items? Who else knows about this?"

"Fortunately, the reports from American Express were being forwarded to me while the finance manager's position was being filled. The charges were about 45 days old when I was notified, and I still need to check to see if Pete's submitted any expense reports. I don't think he did. I called American Express and found out there's a balance of $1,000 outstanding on Pete's account."

"Has Judy Marshall been notified?" I asked. Judy is typically on the road at least three days a week, but she happened to be in the office all this week.

At that moment, his assistant knocked on the door. Larry motioned for her to come it. She looked at me apologetically and handed Larry a manila envelope. "The report you were waiting for just came in," she said. Larry seemed fretful and pulled it from her hand. I couldn't help but wonder how she puts up with this man. At least we pay her well. I decided to excuse myself for a moment and go find Judy. Larry nodded in agreement, anxious to read the report he'd just received.

I stepped out of the conference room and headed down the hall, rushing to catch Judy as she was coming out of her office and hoping she wasn't off to a meeting. She greeted me with her warm smile, "Hi,

Maryanne. I was just going to get some coffee." *Perfect timing,* I thought as I walked down to the kitchen with her.

Tentatively, I touched her forearm. "Thanks, I can use a cup of tea. Judy, do you have a few minutes to meet with Larry and me?" Guardedly, I shared there was something going on in Nashville we needed to discuss but didn't want to risk anyone overhearing the details. As we left the break room, I steered Judy into her office for a moment so I could fill her in on the details before we joined Larry.

Exasperated, she let out a heavy sigh. "I've been sensing some tension between Pete and Kenesha. I've known from the beginning their management styles were so different. I've seriously been thinking of going to Ralph and suggesting Pete was no longer adding value and give him a package to leave. This may be the perfect out."

Walking to the conference room, I said, "Let's not get ahead of ourselves. I want to get to the bottom of this." I opened the door to see Larry had once again taken his seat at the head of the table. "I've briefed Judy, Larry. My thought is she and I need to go down to Nashville. I'd like to look over the reports from American Express first. We've got strict rules that employees can't intentionally use the corporate credit card for personal expenses, and charges like these certainly appear intentional."

Both Larry and Judy looked at me. "Are you suggesting we fire him?" asked Larry cautiously. "I thought we had him on a retained contract."

"I'm not suggesting anything until we have all of the facts. We can't accuse him of credit card fraud if he's been paying the bills, but we do have evidence he's likely breached a rule from your department, Larry. I'd have to review his contract with both Valerie London and outside counsel before we proceed with any action. Judy suggested buying out his contract. We have no precedent for doing so which could be an advantage.

Something for legal review. Whatever action we take, we have to consider the impact on the rest of the staff, like the store managers who reported to him before the transition. And we have to brief Kenesha. She'll need to be part of the decision."

"And you realize this situation is going to test Kenesha—it may break her—despite all the money we're wasting on her coaching." I felt my jaw tighten as I clenched my fist. He wanted to wear my resistance down.

Judy quickly interrupted, "Larry, let's stay focused on Pete. His behavior appears to be at the center of this mess."

"Just how soon can you get down there, Maryanne? Can you leave tomorrow?" Larry was anxious.

Judy was tapping her fingernails against the table. "Hold on. I've got a trip scheduled down there next week. It might be better if Maryanne and I went down together on Monday and treated this like a scheduled visit. While we don't want to lose time, I don't want to raise suspicions. Is there evidence of any additional charges, Larry?"

"No, just those. I'll have copies of the AmEx report made and get any of Pete's expense reports since these charges were made. Both of you are better at these people issues, so I guess I'll let you handle them." It wasn't often Larry conceded, but I was glad he gave up this battle.

As we were getting up to leave, Larry turned to me and said, "Can you hang on for another minute? I've got another problem to discuss with you, Maryanne."

After Judy left, he handed me the manila envelope his assistant had brought in. As I took it from his hand, I jokingly said, "Not another credit card issue, I hope."

"I'm afraid it is, Maryanne. It involves someone else."

I removed the papers from the envelope and saw it was a credit card report from Visa detailing charges made by one of our administrative assistants. We give them each a Visa card to use for incidental business purchases, which is more cost effective than processing expense reports. We have a different arrangement with the Visa cards—the monthly reports come directly to the company. With American Express, the employee is responsible for paying the bills and then is reimbursed for charges. On rare occasions, a personal charge would show up on the Visa invoices, but it had always proved to be a mistake—someone inadvertently pulled the wrong card from their wallet. These were never for large amounts, and we usually forgave them. This time it appeared someone went on a shopping spree one weekend and intentionally used the company Visa card. He hadn't been with the company very long—maybe six or eight months—and worked in one of the departments that reported to Larry. Now I understood why his temperament had changed on the Nashville issue. He needed my help. The report showed a balance of over $1,500 on his credit card for a series of charges all made at different stores in the Woodfield Mall in Schaumburg on the same Saturday.

"Larry," I said, "I'd like Kyle to handle this one. It appears we have enough evidence to terminate him, but we still need to investigate. He should be given the opportunity to explain."

"I knew you'd say that. I just want to keep this as quiet as possible. You're aware how things can get out."

"I understand, Larry. But you've seen that Kyle has proven he can be very discreet. Should we decide termination is the course we're going to take, have you given any thought to prosecuting this employee to recoup the damages?"

"Let me talk it over with Valerie. With the legal fees, it might cost less to just let it go." Larry handed me both the reports.

"I'll ask Kyle to make a copy of the Visa report and return the original to you," I said as I got up to leave. "Thanks Maryanne," he mumbled as rose from the chair and followed me out.

When I got back to my office, I locked the Visa report in my desk. Kyle was attending an all-day seminar, so I sent him a text him to see me first thing tomorrow morning. Then I picked up the phone to call Jason Edison from my networking group. We'd retained him to be Kenesha's executive coach. I knew he couldn't disclose any of their discussions, it would breach confidentiality, but I had a sense there was an underlying issue to this Pete Jackson situation. I wanted to share some insights with him and see if he could give me a reality check. Hopefully, I could catch him for lunch.

"Maryanne, great to hear from you. And I'd love to catch up over lunch." His cheerful disposition always lifted your spirits. "It's been a while since I've eaten at Kings, I must confess." I was sorry to disappoint him, but I suggested meeting at The Gage near Millennium Park. I didn't want to have this conversation in one of our restaurants.

* * *

As the waiter brought our soups and salads, I had just finished bringing Jason up to date on the Nashville situation and my thoughts about what might be behind Pete's actions. "You're right, Maryanne. I can't tell you details about my conversations with Kenesha other than she's well aware of the challenges in this new region, and she's stepping up with confidence. You've always had good instincts about people and situations, so my advice is to follow them. You need to confront Pete with the evidence, but I'd suggest you talk to Kenesha first. Let her tell you firsthand about the working relationship between the two of them."

There was steam coming from Jason's bowl of soup. He winced as he tasted it. It was hot so he picked up his fork and started nibbling on his salad. A pensive look came over his face. "Maryanne, you may not remember this situation that happened back in the consulting firm. Marty Baker, the CFO, got a call from American Express advising they were cancelling the corporate card for an employee. He had reached his limit and was behind in his payments. As usual, his unit couldn't live without him. His boss argued he was some hot-shot systems integrator. They wanted to give him cash advances so he could keep traveling and complete a critical project. Marty was furious—in fact, he discovered they'd already made one advance."

"Come to think of it, Jason, I think I remember hearing some rumors about this. What happened next?"

"Marty wanted to sit down with him and his manager—fire the employee immediately. I had to talk Marty down. We met with the manager first and explained that without a corporate credit card, the employee didn't have the ability to travel, a requirement of his job. We also explained we couldn't afford to keep him on the bench without producing billable hours. The manager was adamant that they wanted him on the project, but Marty held his ground. At that point I suggested we needed to find out what was going on with the employee."

"Did you?"

"Yes. His manager and I sat down with him and during the discussion the employee went from being defensive to pleading to save his job. Seemed he had a gambling problem his wife didn't know about.

He'd maxed out his personal credit cards then started taking advances on his corporate card to cover his gambling debt. We laid it out for him. He'd obstructed his ability to travel because of his gambling debts. If he couldn't travel, he couldn't produce billable hours—there were no local clients at the time. With no billable hours, we couldn't retain him. Then his manager presented an option. One of the universities in the area was looking for an IT professional to help develop a new curriculum, and his background fit their needs. We would see if we could loan him to the university. In addition to helping them with the curriculum, maybe pick up a class or two to teach. If we could work this out, we'd put him on an unpaid leave for a semester, but he'd have to go to the EAP and undergo credit counseling and get help for his problem. His gambling problem was eroding any value he brought to the firm."

Jason didn't have to say anything further to me. I knew it was important to get to the underlying issue in Nashville to plot the right course of action. Just then the waiter came to clear away our dishes and ask if we wanted anything else. "Just the check," I said, and gave Jason a look that implied don't even think of getting this one. "This was very helpful, Jason, especially your insights on the credit card misuse. I'll be flying to Nashville with Judy Marshall on Monday. Now I know how to sequence the series of meetings I'm going to need to have."

* * *

Judy and I returned from Nashville the following Wednesday evening. What an interesting trip. I'd met with Kenesha first under the guise of discussing staffing issues and transition from an HR perspective. Just as I suspected, when I started asking questions about Pete Jackson, I sensed tension. He was hindering the transition process in major ways, including attempting to insert himself into hiring decisions. She'd graciously thank him for his input but move forward with her decisions. It was clear from what both Kenesha and Judy had shared, Pete was resentful he was not offered the District Manager's position, and his resentment was probably the underlying issue.

Before meeting with Pete in the afternoon, Judy and I briefed Kenesha about what had happened. Her shoulders fell as she sighed. "If we decide to terminate him, do we have your buy-in?" Judy asked.

Kenesha's face lit up. "Yes, absolutely."

Pete was surprised, no shocked, I was in the meeting. Judy wasted no time in presenting him with the evidence of the credit card misuse. He immediately got defensive. "There was a late afternoon staff meeting and afterwards I took some of the guys out for dinner—y'know, team building, keep morale up after the takeover. Kenesha isn't good at team building with the guys. Isn't that a legitimate business expense?"

"Yes, it is, Pete," Judy said, "but there's more. There were some purchases at a package store a few days later, and…"

"Haven't you ever pulled the wrong credit card out of your wallet?" he interrupted. "Wait, did that… Did Kenesha accuse me of something? If she did, I want to talk to Larry and Ralph."

Judy sat straighter in the chair. She was getting her back up. She folded her hands and met Pete's gaze before lowering her voice almost to a whisper. It was interesting to watch her in these confrontational situations. As if she was expecting his defensive attitude, she continued. "Pete, I'm going to lay out all of our concerns and then you'll have the opportunity to respond to each. Let me finish, and please refrain from interrupting. You. Will have. Your turn. To speak."

That Bitch!

Pete glanced around the room, scowling, as Judy continued speaking. "There was a charge for dinner at Hooters. While it's acceptable to have a staff dinner, those are generally held in a Kings restaurant. There are additional charges—more than one—at a local package store and those are of concern. There was a cash advance for close to $400. Finally, there was a charge made at Pure Gold Crazy Horse for over $2,000. As we've advised all our managers, the company has a strict rule about personal expenses not being put on the corporate card. So, let's start with Hooters." She was unwavering.

Still on the defensive, Pete didn't let his guard down. He tried to deny he was ever told staff dinners had to be held at a Kings restaurant, adding the guys wanted a change of scenery. *Poor choice of words, Pete.* He also denied he was ever informed about the credit card rules, claiming Kenesha was very lax in explaining things to him. Wrong, Pete. The entire management team was given a briefing by HR, Finance, and Purchasing. Kenesha was part of those briefings. Judy and I were quietly taking down notes.

"Care to explain the charge at the gentlemen's club and cash advance, Pete," Judy said in a steady voice. I could tell she was losing her patience, but not her cool. Suddenly he stood up so abruptly, I thought his chair would fall over. Judy was quick on her feet to meet him, motioned to his chair and said, "Please. Sit. Down. Until we're finished."

He pulled the chair away from the table, sat down, crossed his arms, and went on to explain that over drinks at Hooters they decided to have a bachelor party for one of the assistant store managers. They decided on Crazy Horse to give him one last *male adventure* before he had to settled down, but he didn't expect *you ladies* to understand. The cash advance was for tips.

181

I'd been letting Judy do most of the questioning, but decided it was time to chime in. "Can you explain why you used your corporate card, Pete?" I was waiting for him to say it was a legitimate business expense, team building or something, but he had the good sense not to go that route.

"If my wife saw these charges on the personal card, she often pays the bills, I'd have some explaining to do at home. I don't see what the big deal is. I've paid the charges." He was holding his ground and clearly not giving us any indication that he believed he'd done anything wrong.

After a few more minutes of questioning, Judy ended the meeting and told him to stay in the building until he'd heard more from us. Then we called Ralph and Valerie to go over what we'd learned.

"Ralph, I'm convinced Pete's been deliberately trying to undermine Kenesha and dragging Kings down along the way," said Judy.

"What do you mean?" said Ralph, his tone sharpening.

"Throughout the discussion he tried to place blame on Kenesha. She wasn't clear with instructions. She didn't understand how to build a team. It was obvious he wanted her out so we'd retain him. He was very cavalier in his attitude about his choice of places to *entertain* with the corporate card."

That didn't sit well with Ralph who was furious by now. "That's totally against the corporate culture. Kings is a family restaurant chain. Taking the staff to Hooters and strip clubs reflects poorly on our reputation."

Valerie supported terminating his contract since he'd breached its terms, but I knew she was concerned about subsequent litigation. "Valerie, can we go with Judy's approach and buy him out of the contract which is probably cheaper than litigation? We can still get him off the premises tomorrow," I said. Both Valerie and Ralph agreed.

By this time, it was almost 5:00. Judy contacted Pete and told him we wanted to meet with him again tomorrow morning. In the meantime, I called Kyle and asked him to have Pete's termination paperwork ready for the next morning. Judy alerted IT to suspend his access to the network tomorrow morning after 9, and she arranged with finance to have his American Express card cancelled in the morning. Fortunately, his outstanding balance was now less than $500.

We met with Pete at 9:00 am on Wednesday. Judy informed him she'd discussed the situation with Ralph, and they made the decision we were honoring the financial terms of his retainer agreement. However, his services were no longer needed, and he must leave the premises today. Security would accompany him to his office so he could remove his personal effects. Fortunately, when the sale was finalized, Kenesha moved into his office and he was given a temporary one—something he was not happy about—to limit his access to any company information that may have been in the files. Judy told him he'd continue to receive payments under the terms of his retainer agreement, which was only in effect for another 60 days. He turned his gaze to me and asked about outplacement or other support.

"Pete, you knew once the sale closed, your position with Kings was for a limited time period. It was documented in your retainer agreement. You had adequate time to prepare and do a job search."

"Can I at least talk to Ralph?" he asked me.

"Pete, you're free to place a call to Ralph after you leave. He can decide if he wants to take the call from you."

Resigned, he picked up his pen and quickly finished his out-pro-cessing paperwork. I called security, and he was off the premises within a half hour. Meanwhile, Kenesha and Judy had a conference call with all the store managers in the region to advise them this was Pete's last day. Most were aware his position with Kings was temporary but were unaware of the precise terms of his agreement. To keep speculation under control, Judy explained the transition was moving according to plan, and operationally the region was meeting its targets. She and Ralph decided Pete's services was no longer necessary.

When I got into the office on Thursday—it was last Thursday this all started—I had to meet with Kyle first thing. I wanted to brief him about the Nashville situation, and let him know I wanted to schedule a briefing with the management team there. While Kings wasn't a large corporation, we were larger than any company many of the managers who recently joined us had worked for in the past. We wanted them to understand we take pride in our company's values, and if they gather together outside work at another establishment, it could be perceived as a Kings' sponsored event. Accountability and integrity are key values at Kings. I also wanted a review of the key policies with them.

"Do you think Pete learned some lessons about being a sexist?" Kyle asked. "I mean, did he think he wouldn't get fired because of it?"

"You know, Kyle, it wasn't his sexist attitude—or any of his beliefs—that led Kings to take this action. It was how he acted on his attitudes while representing Kings and conducting Kings' business. His so-called team building and the escapade at the strip club using the corporate card gave the perception it was a Kings' business event. Remember as a company, we can't change or control people's attitudes or beliefs, but we can influence and control their behavior. It was Pete's behavior which led us to take the action we did."

Kyle had a great deal to brief me about. He'd met with Ray, the administrative assistant from the finance department. It seems he was upset because he believed his salary was less than one of the other assistants, so he decided to make up for it with a shopping spree. Larry signed off on the termination and actually sat in on the meeting. Kyle was in the middle of telling me how the meeting went when there was a brisk knock on the door.

"Excuse me," I said, rising to see who it was, but before I could get to the door, it was opened and Larry was standing there with a devilish grin on his face. "Oh good, Kyle's with you. Can I interrupt for a moment?"

"Please come in, Larry. Kyle was just briefing me about the termination."

"Well, here's the final chapter. After talking with Valerie and Ralph yesterday, we decided it wouldn't be worth the time and money prosecuting. We'd probably never recoup the money anyway. I called his house this morning to tell him we weren't going to bring charges. Rick, his partner, husband, whatever, answered the phone and informed me he wasn't there. Then Rick asked me if we were going to prosecute and before I could get a word in, he started begging me not to and exclaimed. 'I told that bitch not to bite the hand that feeds him.' Honestly, I don't know how you two can deal with all this drama," he said chuckling as he headed out the door.

"Some days I don't know how we deal with drama either," I said.

Kyle looked at me shaking his head. "Does Larry realize he's part of our everyday drama?"

I just smiled and thought *Kyle's learning*.

CHAPTER 15

Shaky Starts

"No way," said my sixteen-year-old daughter Erin. "That idiot really didn't say that. And then he offered her the job?"

Erin was reacting to a story I was telling Jack. He was delivering a seminar on the legal approach to hiring, and I'd polled my network for practical examples for him. He wanted to add some realism to his presentation, but some of the stories I'd gotten were quite *unbelievable*.

Just then, Emily, Erin's twin sister, bounced into the kitchen. "What'd I miss?" She never stood still—even before breakfast on a lazy Saturday morning.

"Good. You're just in time to set the table. I'll fill you in once we sit down."

Jack was busy chopping peppers and onions for his favorite omelets. Saturday morning breakfast was a tradition in our house, one that was slowly slipping away as the twins got older. So, when we had a chance, we took it. The girls and I enjoyed sitting at the kitchen table, sipping juice and coffee, and watching Jack cook. Ever since I gave him lessons at the local culinary school, he considers himself quite the chef.

When everything was ready and we started to eat, I continued the story I'd been telling Jack and Erin earlier.

"So, this young woman was so flattered when she was approached by a competing firm and asked to interview for a consulting position. She thought things were going really well during the interview with one of the senior partners. He'd asked her some great interview questions, and they were having what she thought was a very substantive conversation. Out of the blue, he leaned across his desk and said, 'You have really beautiful eyes.'"

"I hope she said something to the jerk," Erin said reaching for a piece of toast.

"She was pretty shaken and didn't know what else to do so she went on talking about the project she was currently working on as if he hadn't said it. He seemed to catch himself and didn't say anything else that was out of line. The interview got back on track and before she left, he offered her the job."

"So, what did she do then?" Emily blurted.

"OMG," sighed Erin. "Don't tell me. She went to work for the jerk."

Rolling her eyes, Emily shouted, "That's insane—why, why, why?"

"I'm right, aren't I, Mom?" responded Erin. "She went to work for the jerk."

"Hold on, girls," I said. "Sometimes there's more to a situation than what's on the surface. And I haven't finished the story."

I went on to explain the woman also saw this offer as a fantastic opportunity and a positive career step. However, she couldn't let that remark go, but she didn't want one comment to influence her decision. After giving it some thought and talking with some people she trusted, she decided to accept the job, but not before she called the partner and told him she didn't appreciate the comment he made. He admitted that he had been wrong and apologized.

"What he said was unfortunate, but it isn't an example of overt harassment. If he'd meant anything more blatant, her stepping up and saying something to him certainly put a stop to any further similar behavior. Sometimes we have to make decisions to do things that make us uncomfortable, and I'm sure it was uncomfortable for her to confront him—especially when she wanted the job. But that was certainly a better choice than walking away from a good opportunity or worse, taking the job and enduring a jerk. Your dad and I want you both to know that you should never, never settle for a job or work for anyone who makes you feel uncomfortable."

We'd finished breakfast, and the girls got up to do their part—clean up and load the dishwasher—when Erin asked me if I'd ever personally had issues when interviewing for a new job.

"Yes, I have. There was a simply stunning situation when I was just out of college. The interviewer, who would have been my boss, asked me to continue the interview over dinner, and I agreed. After dinner, he drove me back to his office where my car was parked, and when we got there, he kissed me like it had been a date. Talk about being confused. I really wanted that job but didn't know what to make of his behavior. Fortunately, I talked it over with my parents who told me I'd be crazy to put myself in a situation like that. So, when I received the job offer, I turned it down.

Years later I got to know someone who worked at that company who told me that guy was legendary for pulling that on other women. I am so glad I didn't take that job."

"Good for you, Mom," Erin said, and I must admit I felt pretty good. Sixteen-year-old daughters don't give compliments very often, so I would treasure this moment.

Jack, who had been sitting quietly taking this all in, asked if we wanted to hear an example he'd heard from a former colleague. The girls, eager to be done with clean up, came back to the table while I poured more coffee.

"She'd been interviewing with a law firm that required potential employees to meet with an industrial psychologist to see if they'd be a cultural fit. The drive to the appointment took her through a residential community. Odd, but not too unusual, until she arrived at the address and saw it was a home. She hesitated, then rang the bell. A woman came to the door and directed her to go around the back to the garage. As she approached the garage, she saw a tall man in shorts and a tee shirt spraying insecticide on his flower garden. He put down the can and introduced himself as the psychologist and welcomed her to his office—inside the garage. She was a bit shocked at this—a home office is one thing, but a garage office was a first for her."

I was thinking I'd be horrified at the situation. "Was the law firm aware of this so-called office setting?" As an HR professional, I thought it was a very unlikely environment to conduct any business, especially a professional interview. And the law firm should know better.

As he pressed a fist to his mouth, I knew Jack was trying to suppress a laugh. "Oh, it gets better. The garage had a large oil spot where the car had been and was filled with garden tools, pots, bags of fertilizer. But in one corner there was a desk sitting in front of a small window that hadn't been washed in decades. There were two chairs in front of the desk, and he directed her to sit in one and as soon as she did, she almost fell out of the chair as it tipped forward. She quickly recovered and as she put her purse down on the floor, she noticed that the front legs of the chair she was sitting in were shorter than the back legs—no wonder she'd almost fallen out. She remembered hearing about people who used techniques like this to test the applicant, so she was on her guard."

"I hope she sued the jerk," Erin interrupted.

"The psychologist sat behind the desk which had a large lamp on one corner. He turned on the light and at first, she thought that was a good idea since the window wasn't letting in much light but then quickly realized the way the shade was tilted, she was staring into the light. She'd been a psych major in college and remembered that this was what was called a *stress interview*—the shaky chair incident, the light in her eyes— all designed to see how she handled difficult situations."

"Like sitting in a garage isn't difficult enough to pass the stress test," sighed Emily.

"Now that she knew what was going on, she relaxed a bit. The interview started out slowly with him asking questions about where she'd grown up and about her family. He didn't ask anything about her law school experiences except to inquire if she'd dated a lot in college. This led into some very uncomfortable territory for her as a woman and as an attorney."

Jack paused to take a sip of coffee, expecting more comments from the twins. Emily was rolling her eyes as Erin was sneaking peeks at her phone, thinking I didn't see her.

"Well," continued Jack. "He started asking her questions which she knew were totally inappropriate if not illegal. And she was an attorney, and he was contracting with a law firm to do these interviews. One of the questions he asked her was what was the most she'd ever weighed in her life—and she was very tall and thin. I think the last question was the final straw. He asked her why she wasn't married."

Before Jack could finish, the twins and I were laughing at the idea of this professional woman sitting in a garage being asked such ridiculous questions.

"Don't tell me *she* went to work for a law firm that used that idiot," squealed Erin.

"Yes, she did," said Jack giving Erin a playful nudge, "but not without telling the managing partner what she'd experienced during her interview. And very shortly thereafter, the firm decided not to use that psychologist's services again. So, there are lots of ways to change the world."

I started thinking about some of the other funny interview experiences I've heard of over the years. I told the girls about a colleague I had years earlier who interviewed for an HR position in a very large company. The interviewer was a young, good looking man and my friend thought the interview was going really well when he told her she wouldn't be moving forward in the interview process. She was devastated until later that day when he called her and asked her out for dinner that weekend. They've been married for over 20 years, and she's forgiven him for not hiring her.

"You had an unusual interview once," said Jack, "the one where they asked you to interview yourself?"

Emily giggled when I said, "Yes, I'd almost forgotten that one. I had been in HR at Kings for just a short time and one of our competing restaurant companies lured me in for an interview for a director level job. I was flattered. The interview was over dinner in their best restaurant, so at least I knew I'd get a good meal. The vice president was there along with three other men. We were escorted by the host to a large circular booth and they put me in the middle with two men on either side of me."

I stopped to take a sip of coffee.

"We ordered dinner and then the VP said since I was in HR, why didn't I interview myself. I must have looked shocked, so he said I should just ask myself questions and answer the questions. It was so ridiculous that I knew I had to pull myself together first. So, I made two of the men get up to let me out of the booth, and I rushed to the rest room and laughed and laughed until I realized I had to go back and continue the interview."

Erin and Jack were smirking when Emily said, "Mom, what did you do when you got back to the table?"

"Well, I did what they'd requested. I asked myself a question and then I answered it. Before too long, it was obvious to these clueless men this wasn't the way to conduct a professional interview. One of them suggested we eat our dinner and reschedule for another time. I agreed knowing there was no way I would ever see them again *and* there was no way I would ever work for that company."

"I've had some interesting experiences in interviews myself, Jack said. "Once I was conducting an interview and I asked what I thought was a perfectly reasonable question and the man burst into tears. I don't mean he had tears in his eyes—he was crying his eyes out. I didn't know what to do, so I said I would leave and come back in a few minutes. When I returned with a box of tissues, he had himself under control."

Realizing I was watching her, Erin averted her eyes away from her phone. "What did you ask him that upset him so much?"

"I think it was a question I often ask—what do you consider your greatest achievement?"

"But Dad," said Emily, "Why would that make him cry?"

"Well, most people answer that question by talking about something they've done in their professional career, but he started talking about his children and how they were his greatest achievement. Guess what, we hired him, and he was a great addition to our firm. I must admit that experience was a little overwhelming for me—you all know how I don't deal well with tears."

I leaned over and patted his hand to let him know we were aware of what a sensitive guy he was and lightened the mood by saying…

"And then there are the great moments in interviewing that are so funny but as the interviewer you can't laugh. I remember asking an applicant a very typical interview question—tell me about yourself. She looked horrified by the question, thought for a few seconds and said, 'Well, I love shoes. I have hundreds and hundreds of pairs of shoes. I love buying them and I love wearing them. I love looking at them in my closet. In fact, I had a special closet built to keep them all. I keep them in clear plastic boxes so I can see them all, and they're kept dust free. I have winter shoes, and I have summer shoes. I have designer shoes, and I have everyday shoes.' She couldn't seem to stop herself. And she must have seen my face as I was doing my best not to laugh. No lie, this went on for what seemed to be minutes—her sharing her love for shoes. Now if loving shoes had been a job requirement, she would have probably been hired but it wasn't the case, so she wasn't hired—no surprise there."

Shaky Starts

All of these stories got me thinking that I needed to check with our talent acquisition team at Kings to review our hiring procedures. It is so important for each person we interview, whether we hire them or not, to have a good experience. Every applicant is a potential customer, and we want to maintain our reputation as a great place to work as well as a great place to eat.

CHAPTER 16

Fantasies

I don't know how many times I've said if you shock easily, you won't succeed in HR. This was no exception. When I arrived at work this cold, Chicago morning, Bob Zimmerman was waiting outside my office holding a cup of coffee in each hand. Once we walked inside and sat down, he handed a cup to me. With a sheepish smile he said, "I had a call from IT late last night, and you need to help me with what to do next." I knew this wasn't going to be good.

In the four years since he's been our COO, I've never known Bob to be rattled by any situation, and he deals with many when Ralph is out of the office visiting the restaurants. Now he seemed unsure about something, and it was unusual.

I grabbed the cup to have something to warm my hands as I listened intently to Bob.

"IT was doing their usual nightly backup and found what appears to be porn posted on one of our servers. When they checked further, they found it came from one of the computers here in the building—one assigned to a young woman in purchasing. As head of IT, Brian Chang thought we should bring this to you to help us sort out next steps."

Obviously uncomfortable, Bob could hardly make eye contact with me and was flipping a pen back and forth as he spoke. Unusual since he's brought a real level of professionalism to our Leadership Team. He and I work really well together. It isn't every COO who understands the value HR brings to the organization, but Bob gets it. We almost always see things the same way. His support for me and my team has really solidified HR as a valued partner to all the restaurants.

When I heard it was a woman's computer, I had what I think is a typical reaction—usually men are the ones who fall prey to this kind of behavior—but then I checked myself. I try to always reserve judgment until all the facts are in. Still, I wondered *Could it have been a guy using a woman's desktop?* Bob shared what he knew, and we were both surprised. I said, probably not for the last time today, "What's wrong with people?"

I went to get more coffee and stopped to see if Kyle was free to meet with us. He said he was finishing a report on an employee relations issue he'd just mediated and would be right in. When he joined us, Bob filled him in, and I asked him to get with Brian in IT. We needed the details before we could determine next steps.

"This is a priority, Kyle. I need to hear back from you and Brian asap."

After Kyle and Bob left my office, I sat back to think about how my days never seem to go as planned. On my agenda today was a review of the analytics we needed to complete the workforce plan that would be part of the total budget for the organization, but it would get sidelined. Employee issues don't wait, and this one had the potential of being particularly messy.

Kyle returned in a few minutes with a clearly uncomfortable Brian in tow who was carrying a bottle of water. "Brian's filled me in on what happened, but I think you need to hear this firsthand so, Brian, over to you."

"Well, during our routine back up this issue surfaced, and our policy says we have the right to monitor any use of our computers at any time."

"Brian," I replied with a slight smile, "That's policy, so please don't think your team did anything wrong."

"Thanks, Maryanne," he said taking a sip of water. "But now that I've seen the photos in question, I am not as upset as I was when I first heard about it. The person wasn't downloading porn from the internet. She was posting pictures of herself to an external site."

My heart stopped. "What kind of pictures?"

Kyle responded before Brian could speak. "They're pictures of her wearing very little clothing."

We needed to bring Larry Blackstone into this discussion since purchasing reports to him, and then we needed to meet with the woman and find out what her story was. Kyle volunteered to brief Larry, and I decided to wait till he returned to call the woman. I'm so proud that Kyle is offering to have these conversations with the Leadership Team. He's gaining so much confidence.

Waiting for Kyle, I thought how Larry can soft-pedal issues involving his people. This time I suspected he'd probably not want to get too involved given the issue's sensitive nature. While I appreciate Larry's support of his people, if he goes too far trying to protect them, it can cause serious problems once the facts are all in. I thought, and not for the first time, *I wish Larry would appreciate that while his world of numbers is pretty black and white, my world of people and their behavior has lots of shades of grey.*

Kyle returned to say Larry agreed we had to confront her and wanted to be kept up to date on the story. I thought to myself *he'll let me handle it and then probably tell Ralph I'd messed it up.* Oh well, by now I'm used to how he operates. I picked up the phone, called the woman, and asked her to come to my office right away. I am well aware of the shock waves it sends when the Chief HR Officer personally sends for an employee, but this was potentially serious.

While Kyle and I waited for her, we decided Kyle should take the lead in the meeting. He reminded me who she was. She's fairly new to Kings and now I remembered her from our onboarding session. She'd asked some really good questions at that meeting about the company's values which caught my attention.

A few minutes later, she knocked lightly on my open door. I asked her in and offered her coffee. She declined. Kyle got right into the discussion and told her what had been found on her computer. I honestly thought she was going to tell us someone must have used her computer without her permission. Then all I would have to do was give the lecture about passwords and we would be done. Imagine my surprise when she burst into tears. I handed Kyle the tissue box that is always in every HR office, and he offered it to her. She got herself under control and said, "I am so sorry. I love my job here at Kings and I don't want to lose it, but I entered a contest on the radio to earn some extra money."

Kyle and I looked at each other in confusion. He said, "What does the contest have to do with the pictures of you on your work computer?"

"Well, see, the way you win the contest is to have people vote for you online, and all the other contestants were posting glamour photos on their sites. I don't have the money to get those pictures taken professionally so I thought these pictures would get me some votes and maybe help me win the contest."

"But how did those pictures get on your work computer? Why didn't you use your own personal computer?" Kyle asked.

"Well, see, I only have my iPhone. My computer's old and doesn't connect to the Internet very well. I downloaded the pictures from my iPhone to my work computer so I could upload them to the contest site. I meant to delete them after I'd done that but got interrupted before I could get them off my work computer."

Kyle and I didn't exchange glances, but I know we were both thinking *what's wrong with people*. We thanked her for her honesty but told her she had violated company policy about using our computer system and network for her personal gain and questionable activity. We also advised her IT had blocked the contest site. We sent her back to work and let her know her manager would be speaking with her about next steps.

So many of the decisions we make require using good judgment—even if the employees don't—and this seemed to be one of those times. After talking with her manager and bringing Larry up to speed, we decided not to terminate her even though we could have based on our policy. While it was obvious she did something wrong, her actions didn't put Kings in a bad position and termination wasn't warranted. Instead, we prepared a written warning notice, met with her, and advised that if she did anything like this again she would be terminated.

This provided a good opportunity to do some *just-in-time training* about our IT policies, and I asked Kyle to get with Brian and put some ideas together for me to discuss with the Leadership Team.

Later in the day I called my HR team together and briefed them about this situation, just in case they heard any rumors. Gloria Lincoln, our Employee Benefits Director, could hardly contain her laughter. "Maryanne, I'm sorry and I know this isn't funny, but it reminded me of when I worked at the TV station earlier in my career. We had an on-air weather guy who was caught looking at porn while we were on the air. He and the news anchors all sat at the same long desk and after his weather segment, he'd go back to his favorite sites with his co-workers sitting within feet of him. We found out when someone just happened to walk behind him and saw what was on his monitor. He was fired immediately and was so surprised, protesting he wasn't hurting anyone. Not only was it against station policy to use company equipment to access porn, we reminded him, but he was doing this during a live broadcast. And didn't he realize if he hit the wrong button while on the air, we'd all be in more than a bit trouble with the FCC? That had never occurred to him."

I noticed Kyle looking at Noelle Livingston, our Training and Development Director, before suggesting our onboarding process may need updating. "Maybe employees don't understand our policies or maybe we need to emphasize our IT policies a bit more." He proposed doing a video of Brian talking about the policy. While it would be ideal to invite Brian into onboarding meetings at our corporate headquarters to discuss policy and other IT issues, if he weren't available, the video would be shown. It could also be used in our regional offices for onboarding and for an employee refresher training. Noelle said she'd work with Brian and Kyle on the video while they were preparing the training that would go out to all staff members.

"Let's make sure to emphasize accountability—actions have con-sequences. Let me give you an example," I said as I went on to share a story from Stephanie Packard which turned out to be very sad. There was a custodian at the college where she worked who had been there for well over 20 years. He had two kids enrolled in the college, since employees were eligible for free tuition for their dependents. He was well liked and always reliable. One day a department head was walking down a corridor and heard noise coming from what he knew was an empty classroom. He opened the door to find the custodian sitting at a desk with his feet up on another desk while very graphic pornography was blasting from the flat screen monitor.

I stopped for a minute to look around at my usually talkative staff and saw they were all staring at me in amazement. "The custodian jumped up and looked for the remote and quickly turned off the movie or whatever it was, but the damage was done. He told the department head it had been on when he came in to clean, and he was trying to turn it off. But since he'd been sitting watching it with his feet up, obviously that was a lie."

Noelle, who had diligently been taking notes looked up and turned to me. "That must have been a difficult situation since he'd been a good employee for so long. You said it had a sad ending. What happened?"

I explained he was terminated, and his kids lost their free tuition which was the really heartbreaking part for everyone who was part of the decision. The termination was based on his violation of the policy and his incredibly poor judgment.

"Think of it this way," I said. "What might have happened if students had come into that room instead of the department head—that would have been something. Fortunately, we haven't had too many problems at Kings with employees accessing porn, or other questionable sites, from work computers. Why do people think they can get away with this?"

"Because they can't do it at home." said Gloria. "A colleague recently shared an example of this."

She went on to tell the tale of a bunch of guys who started a challenge—whoever shared the most nude photos of women got his drinks paid for by the others at the next two happy hours. The idea was they'd share these photos on their smartphones during break, but the competition got so intense, this one guy started sending porn from his personal device to his colleagues at their work email addresses. His defense—he was initiating the emails from his own device, not the company's, so he wasn't breaking any policy.

"Obviously, this genius, didn't realize he was sending stuff over the company's network, which is company property," said Gloria.

"Gloria," I said, "that reminds me of another one I heard about IT surveillance uncovering porn sites being accessed from a female employee's computer. In their experience, it is highly uncommon for women to access porn at work, so they went to her with what they'd uncovered."

"She was horrified when they confronted her and extremely adamant that she'd never accessed those sites. They put a camera in her office and quickly discovered a guy was going into her office after hours and once he had figured out her password, was sitting at her desk watching porn on her computer..." I paused for dramatic effect, "while he was—Kyle, what did you call it—*pleasuring himself*. But that wasn't the best part—the guy who was caught worked in the IT department and helped develop the computer usage policy. When confronted, he said he was doing *research*. Of course, he was fired immediately."

A blank stare came over Ryan's face. "I don't get it. Why didn't he just use his phone and live stream?"

"This was probably awhile back, Ryan, and live streaming wasn't here yet," Gloria chuckled. "Right Maryanne?"

Trying to suppress a laugh, I nodded in agreement.

Ryan still looked puzzled as he said, "Here's another one I don't get—email stalking. A buddy of mine in IT told me about a guy sending emails to woman saying things like 'I dream about you every night. You are naked and so beautiful.' Or 'I picture you coming home from work and taking off all your clothes.'"

"That's creepy," Kyle said, "and stupid. How did the company find out? Did she tell anyone?"

"It took her awhile, but yes, she finally told a co-worker. She'd been terrified to talk about it, fearing the guy would overhear her and say something at work. The co-worker told her to go to management. HR and the CEO called the guy in and confronted him with the emails—which fortunately, the woman hadn't deleted. The guy pleaded to keep his job saying she was so beautiful that he couldn't help himself and promised he'd never do it again. But the company fired him and wouldn't let him come back."

"I had to work with IT at my last company on a stalking issue that also involved emails," said Leslie Hernandez our HRIS Director. "It started innocently—this male director was always calling a female associate in the accounting department across town, and the conversations seemed all business-like, at first. Then one day he asked her what she was wearing, and she laughed. They were moving offices, and she told him she was wearing shorts and a t-shirt that day. He wanted to know if they were short shorts and a short, tight shirt. That sent up a red flag for her, and she ended the conversation quickly. When she stopped being friendly on the phone, he started sending her emails—always describing what he imagined her wearing. Fortunately, after she received the second email, she forwarded it to me to create a trail and told me about the phone conversations. IT confirmed it was coming from the director—he was using a personal email account like the guy sending porn to his buddies' work email accounts. While IT and my HR Director were deciding on a course of action, he sent another email—this one more graphic than the first two."

"What happened?" asked Gloria.

"Big shock. The director's boss was in denial, wanted to elevate it to the CEO. But with the emails as proof, HR Director and the General Counsel, both men by the way, were adamant that we had to terminate this guy. They didn't want anyone else subjected to this type of behavior at work. And the General Counsel made a good point about workplace violence. He didn't want to risk this guy retaliating or making threats against the woman."

As I looked around the table at my talented team, I could tell there were more stories to share on this topic, but our time was up. We would pick this up again—I had no doubts about that.

CHAPTER 17

Criminal Minds

Unfortunately, our workplaces are, at times, threatened by dark and violent behavior. As HR professionals, this is our biggest challenge. It haunts us at times. How can signs of aberrant behavior be recognized and reported? Have we done enough to guard against this behavior? Are there adequate protections in place?

Stephanie Packard sat frozen, looking at the package on her desk. It was stamped all over with the words *Live Ammunition*. *Not again*, she thought, as she suddenly realized her breath had shortened. She took three deep, complete breaths just as she'd learned to do in her meditation class to help her relax.

She ran her fingers over the box. Even though her touch was light, she could feel a stinging sensation in her fingertips. Was she imagining that? The words *Live Ammunition* appeared in her line of sight once again, and she heard the sound. *Bang. Bang.* Then she heard the screams. She shuddered, shook her head, and then looked at the addressee's name. Why did he have this delivered to work? Does he have a gun on the premises? Is he planning something horrific? She slowly turned to the window and looked out across the campus, fighting off the memories from 20 years ago. *I don't ever want to go through that again,* she thought.

She'd been the assistant controller for the bank. To deter robberies, the bank's practice was not to keep a great deal of cash in the branches, and all the branches had bullet resistant glass. She had worked closely with HR to develop practices and procedures involving both departments, in case a robbery did occur. Get a dye pack into the cash if you can, but don't risk your life or the lives of others. Don't get aggressive. All associates who worked in the branches received very specific training on the procedures.

She was in a meeting when the call came. There was a robbery in progress at the Glenview branch. Two robbers had entered the building and one jumped over the counter and pistol whipped the teller. He asked for the money. Another teller quickly complied, gave him the money, and the robber left. An off-duty police officer was outside and witnessed the incident. He alerted the police and apprehended the two robbers in the bank on their way out. Police were immediately on the scene. The robber who jumped the counter pulled out a gun, threatened the police officer, and ultimately lost his life in the ensuing struggle. A third suspect, parked down the street in the get-away car, surrendered when he heard shots fired.

Corporate security and the CEO arrived just as the police had secured the scene and shut the branch down, with the witnesses inside. The paramedics administered to the teller who'd been pistol whipped. She gave a statement before being taken to the hospital for treatment and observation.

Stephanie was struck by the speed with which everything came together that day—reassuring the staff they had done everything perfectly and according to plan, confirming no one else was physically hurt, assessing the degree of trauma those present had undergone, and getting employee assistance program professionals on the scene within one hour for the employees and customers alike.

But trauma lingers. People were aware of post-traumatic stress disorder then, but it wasn't publicly discussed. Some employees refused to return to the same branch, so they were allowed to transfer to others or move into different roles. Customers didn't want to return to the Glenview branch, and the bank saw a decrease in deposits there for several months. No amount of training deters tragedy nor prepares people for it. It wasn't long after this that Stephanie realized solving problems involving people was much more impactful than solving problems involving numbers and directed her career toward HR.

The ringing phone startled Stephanie back into the present. As she reached for the phone, she almost knocked the receiver off its cradle. "Human Resources. Stephanie Packard," she snapped, without looking at the caller ID.

"Stephanie? It's Maryanne. Is everything okay?"

At the sound of her friend's voice, Stephanie felt her shoulders soften as the tension released. "Yes, just dealing with yet another challenge. In fact, Maryanne, is Jack in his office today? I could use a reality check on something before I take this situation to in-house counsel."

Jack often acted as a de facto member of their networking group and took an occasional call from the members if they wanted to bounce a legal issue off of him. Stephanie quickly explained that a box was delivered to the college addressed to the deputy IT director with the words

Live Ammunition stamped all over it. The mailroom supervisor, rather than confront the employee, had the good sense to bring it right to HR. With their vice president currently on leave, Stephanie is the most senior person in the HR department, so the box was delivered to her and now sitting on her desk.

"I want to make sure the course of action I propose to take won't be outside the boundaries of the Firearm Concealed Carry Act," Stephanie explained.

"Yes, Jack's in the office today, and I'm sure he'll be glad to take the call. In fact, I was calling about dinner before the show this Saturday. Does Catch 35 sound good to you? I know Norm loves seafood."

"That sounds great, Maryanne. We can catch up on all this drama on Saturday." Stephanie was finally able to smile. As she dialed Jack's number, she realized while the current situation was serious, she was in a position to avert a potential crisis.

"Jack, thanks so much for taking my call," Stephanie said when he came on the line. "One of these days I'll convince my in-house counsel they need to retain your firm for our employment law needs."

"No problem, Stephanie. Always happy to help a friend."

Stephanie quickly explained the current situation and her concerns with the new law. "Jack, I'm aware the act does not allow individuals with the appropriate license to carry a concealed weapon at colleges. We've posted the required sign issued by the State Police advising concealed weapons are prohibited on the property. But all I can verify at this time is the intent to take possession of ammunition. A concealed weapon may or may not be involved."

"You've done your research, Stephanie," Jack began. "And yes, the college is covered by one of the exceptions. But you know as well as I, laws can be ambiguous until litigation takes place, and case law sets additional standards. Here's what we've been advising our clients. Since the Act doesn't directly address it, it leaves intact an employer's ability to prohibit weapons in the workplace. Whether or not the employer owns the property, it can maintain a ban on weapons simply by virtue of its inherent control of and discretion in the employment relationship. Also, the Act is silent about potential liability from negligence claims for an employer not doing enough to prevent workplace violence by barring guns in the workplace. Stephanie, you've explained the situation, but what is it you'd like to do about it? How do you plan to proceed?"

"Obviously, I want to confront him and find out why he'd do such a thing. I'll need to notify his management and campus security in case it involves more than just ammunition. This could be a larger threat if guns are discovered. Interestingly, Jack, we've long had a policy banning guns and ammunition on the premises—it's a zero-tolerance policy. We've a precedent for terminating people for violating the policy. The individual in this case is a deputy director—he should know better. But I'm always aware of my sensitivity to workplace violence given the situation I was exposed to when I worked at the bank years ago."

"Stephanie, you realize I have to tell you I can't give you legal advice for a number of reasons. I'm not retained to do so and don't know what your policy says explicitly, nor do I know all of the facts in this situation, specifically his position or rationale for having ammunition delivered to the workplace. But I can give you some *friendly advice* if you want a point of view to take to your in-house counsel."

"Jack, that's exactly why I called—for *friendly advice*—a legal reality check if you will."

"Okay, Steph. If you've got a zero-tolerance policy about guns *and* ammunition in the workplace, and if you have precedent for taking adverse action against employees who've violated your policy, I think you've demonstrated you've exercised inherent control of and discretion in the employment relationship. It sounds like you're exercising the General Duty clause under OSHA to provide a workplace free from recognized hazards that are causing or are likely to cause death or serious physical harm through this policy. You want to limit liability from potential negligence claims," Jack concluded.

"That's what I needed to hear—an assurance I'm not off base in my thinking when I talk to in-house counsel. He's great, but not as well-versed in employment law as I'd like him to be. By the way, I spoke with Maryanne before I called you. Norm and I are looking forward to seeing you at dinner and the theatre on Saturday."

"I'll be looking forward to hearing what happened. Good luck, Stephanie," Jack said before he hung up the phone.

* * *

When Jack and I arrived at Catch 35 on Saturday evening, Stephanie and Norm were already there. "So sorry to keep you waiting," I said.

Norm walked over and gave me a big hug. "Ahh, but you didn't. We just got here."

"My sanity check," said Stephanie smiling, as she rushed toward Jack.

The hostess returned, and Norm told her the party was all here. We were quickly seated. Once we settled in, drinks ordered, Jack asked, "So, Stephanie, how did the situation turn out?"

"You're not going to believe this," Stephanie said, sucking in a quick breath. "I called Derek, the VP of Technology, to come to my office and briefed him. Showed him the box with the live ammo. He wanted to confront the employee in his office—which is in another building—with the box of ammo. I told him absolutely not. We're not carrying this around the campus. Besides, for all we knew, the employee could be stockpiling weapons. I insisted we meet in my office."

Stephanie rolled her eyes and took a sip of water. "Seriously. Before we called the employee, Derek and I talked with in-house counsel. We have this young, new lawyer, Harvey, who's pretty sharp. I'd briefed him, laid out what I saw as next steps, and shared your friendly advice. He had an interesting take on the situation. While he agreed with your interpretation of the law, Jack, he pointed out the employee never actually took possession of the ammunition. I sense he sees everything as black or white. He doesn't understand employment law involves people and their actions and the gray areas we deal with. After we hashed it out—I explained it was his intent to take possession of the ammunition which he would have done so except for the good sense of the mailroom supervisor—he decided to withhold judgment until we talked to the employee. He wanted to be in on the meeting, in fact, almost insisted on it. Derek on the other hand was adamantly opposed. He explained to Harvey while this guy is generally even tempered, if he sees a lawyer sitting in the room, it could totally throw him off guard."

She paused for a moment. "I thought it might be good for Harvey to see an employee issue firsthand, but not under these circumstances. I agreed with Derek and deferred to his judgment—he knows his employees best. So, Derek called Ned and told him to meet us in my office. I have to say I had a knot in the pit of my stomach while we were waiting for him. I called the head of security and asked him to sit in our VP's office, which is across from mine, as a precaution. He kept the door slightly open to have a good view of him when he arrived."

I noticed the slow grin forming on Jack's face as he leaned in closer. "Sooooo, what happened when he showed up?"

"He walked in, all happy-go-lucky, and said, 'What's up? Is this about the hire for the computer security analyst?' You can imagine his surprise when he spotted the box sitting on my desk. He was dumbfounded when Derek asked if he cared to explain."

"And his explanation was......" asked Jack.

"It seems he didn't want the package to go to his house—he has little kids," Stephanie continued. "He was planning to keep it in his office until the weekend when he and his brother were going to go target practice near the Wisconsin border. His brother has kids too. He didn't think there was anything wrong with it since he'd have it locked in a file drawer in his office. When we asked if he knew about the policy, he said he thought it meant you couldn't have ammunition *and* a gun—after all, what good was ammo without the gun. Seriously?"

The waiter came with our drinks and Stephanie quickly changed the subject. Norm was just shaking his head and smiling as he took a sip of his bourbon and water. Once the waiter left, Stephanie picked up the story.

"At that point I told him the policy was crystal clear. It states possessing dangerous weapons, including, but not limited to, firearms, explosives including ammunition, knives, etc. was strictly prohibited. The expression on his face was like a deer in the headlights."

"Stephanie," Jack said, "Did he ever receive a copy of the policy? Did he sign for it?"

As Stephanie raised her left eyebrow, I responded, "I've got this," and turned to face Jack. "How many times do we have to have this discussion? It's just not realistic to hand employees a copy of every policy during new-hire orientation and have them sign each one. Even if it was, the employees have to be responsible for reading them. We can't force them to do it. I know you lawyers think having employees sign for a policy is somehow a legal CYA process—but it doesn't guarantee someone will change behavior."

I turned to look at everyone now. "How simple all our jobs would be if the mere existence of workplace policies were enough to eliminate bad or deviant behavior at work. But employee relations is hard."

Stephanie and Norm were nodding in agreement. "So true, Maryanne," she said before turning to Jack.

"All employees receive a copy of the handbook and sign an acknowledgement. And all managers have access to all of the policies. He had plenty of opportunity to read and ask questions. But, back to Ned. He started to protest he didn't have any guns in his office and didn't think this was a big deal."

"No, buts," I told him. "Policy aside, did you consider what it would look like to have a box of live ammo being carried across the campus, especially in light of all the episodes of campus violence? I appreciate your concern for the safety of your young children, but this shows a lack of concern for the safety of the students at the college. And another thing. The college mailroom isn't for your personal use. Imagine if everyone had personal packages delivered to work. It would strain our resources.

It would be the same as if every employee brought their personal computer—their personal property—to you and asked you to fix it."

"I'll bet that got his attention," I said.

"I think it did, Maryanne. Meanwhile, Derek slipped out and placed a call to counsel. Once Harvey heard the employee was planning on keeping the ammo at work for several days, he agreed we had grounds to terminate him."

"It's so sad," I said. "He had young children and now he's out of work."

Stephanie took a sip of her wine. "Interestingly, he hadn't been with the college long—six or eight months, I believe. Derek confided the guy was struggling in the position, not meeting deadlines, etc., and he was working with our VP of HR on a plan of action. It was probably a matter of time until he was terminated."

"Still, to show such poor judgment. What's wrong with people," I exclaimed.

The waiter came over to take our order, and when he left, Jack commented, "I'm glad we got here before it gets too busy. We do have a show to catch."

"Maryanne, do you remember the time I had a client with the employee who was charged with armed robbery?" Jack asked. "I got a call one morning from this client. Apparently, an employee had not shown up for work and later in the morning they got a call from a family member saying he was in jail, arrested the night before for attempted armed robbery. The client wanted to know what to do—wanted to know if they should fire him."

I noticed Stephanie shuddering before she said, "What did you tell them?"

"His actions didn't have anything to do with work. I advised them to put him on an unpaid leave for 30 days and if he didn't return by then, to terminate him at that point based on the expiration of the leave and his inability to be at work. This kept their decision work related and distinct from his outside criminal activity."

"Do you know if they took your advice?"

"They said they did. The dynamic in play in these situations is as soon as there's a mention of crime, violence, or a threat, people grow tense and judgment shuts down. It's always good to prepare for the unexpected in advance of an incident."

"Amen," said Stephanie, who'd been running her fingers around the side of the bread plate. "I often wonder if managers and employees realize policies and procedures aren't developed in a vacuum. It's not as if we have nothing else to do. There are so many of them we hope we never have to use."

I looked over and saw Norm looking intently at the ice in the bottom of his empty glass. Norm had worked many years as a senior manager and then director for a manufacturing company before he retired. "Don't hold back, Mr. Packard. I'm sure you've encountered some interesting situations in your day."

Norm signaled the waiter over and asked for another drink. "Anyone else?" Jack joined him, but Stephanie and I said we'd wait for dinner before getting our second glass of wine. Just then our appetizer arrived. As we all started nibbling on it, Norm began his dark tale.

"First thing on a Monday morning, in the TribLocal section of the Chicago Tribune, is the story of a person arrested for alleged murder in a knife fight. The story identified the person as an employee of the plant—a member of the janitorial staff. I'd just been promoted to director and the facilities department, including the janitors, reported to me. By the time I arrived at work, the whole department, not to mention the rest of the plant, was abuzz with the news. I was called to the President's conference room, along with legal counsel and human resources. One of the first things HR did was to pull the employee's file and check that references had been done—they had. The immediate decision was made—if he didn't show to work or call for three days, he'd be terminated per the policy. This is ultimately what happened. A registered letter was sent to his home advising his employment was being terminated."

By now, Norm was sitting at the edge of his chair drumming his fingers on the table. "In the meantime, though, there was a potential employee relations issue brewing, which I'm sure all of you understand. Other employees, in his department and throughout the plant, were professing, almost demanding, they didn't want him back. Workplace violence had been in the news and employees were asking about security screening for weapons and locker checks. Suddenly, their personal privacy took a back seat to safety. The communications team helped with internal messages—we take personal safety seriously as we do our employee's rights."

With that, our dinners arrived. "Can I get you anything else?" the waiter asked.

"Two more glasses of wine," said Stephanie.

"Both for you?" I joked as he walked away.

"After this week? I probably need two more. Seriously," she chuckled.

"You were lucky, Norm," said Jack. "Unlike my client with the armed robbery situation, your employee didn't call, so you had grounds to terminate him per your policy. But it still left you with the PR issue, both internally with the employees and externally with the media. Your company's name was in the news and not for the best reason. In my client's case, the reason for the employee's absence was not known to the staff. He apparently kept to himself, so co-workers didn't know much about him. There wasn't much external publicity. Folks just assumed he was on a medical leave. In both these circumstances, however, what if the employees had made bail and wanted to come back to work? That can always be a tenuous situation."

"Many of us were holding our breath waiting for those three days to pass," replied Norm. "And media coverage subsided—well, at least is wasn't focused on the plant."

"Did you make the EAP available to the employees?" I asked.

"That was included in the communications, reminding employees the company offered an EAP and they could call and speak to a counselor. We didn't see the need to bring counselors to the plant since nothing occurred on site and the employee never returned to work."

"I don't know how organizations managed in the days before EAPs," I said. "They're such a valuable resource, which reminds me of an interesting encounter I heard about from a colleague."

I went on to tell them about my colleague who was conducting an investigation into sexual harassment for one of their clients. They had concerns about the culprit and his explosive personality, so they took precautions—security nearby, and putting the EAP representative on alert about a possible referral. As predicted, the employee became very agitated during the meeting when he was confronted with the allegations.

He threatened to shoot his kids and any cops that may be nearby. Security immediately intervened, called the police, and restrained him until the cops arrived on the scene. Security also searched his office for his car keys, which miraculously he'd left in his desk drawer. When the police arrived, they searched his car and found guns in his vehicle.

"How did the EAP get involved?" asked Stephanie.

"Many of the employees witnessed the car search and the employee's removal from the premises by the police and were upset. The company arranged to bring the EAP on site in this case, so the employees had easy access to the counselors."

Jack had been listening intently. "It sounds as if they had a good emergency response plan in place. We're always stressing the importance of one with clients. You never know when the unexpected may occur. Have a plan and have training about it—often."

Jack turned to Stephanie and said. "I've been sharing with Maryanne something I've been reading about—workplace threat assessments, a specialty that's emerging within the mental health field. From what I understand, they can provide invaluable advice regarding steps employers could take to manage problematic employees, enhance safety, and diminish the risk of violence. I'm looking into it further and will pass along anything I learn."

I noticed Norm had just reached over to squeeze Stephanie's hand. He'd been pushing her to retire and move to a warmer climate, but Stephanie was resistant. At 62, she still wanted to work a few more years and collect a full retirement. Her daughter and grandchildren were in Chicago, and she wasn't anxious to leave them. "Listen, if you're married to a cop, a firefighter, or other first responder, you live with the looming threat they could be in harm's way every day. But for employees and managers in the industries we work or worked in, it's the farthest thing from your mind," he sighed, squeezing her hand once again.

"It's an unfortunate world we live in today," Stephanie declared as her face suddenly softened. "Fortunately, we live in an area where we have a large selection of good entertainment. I hope you're all in the mood to laugh after this somber dinner conversation. I hear the play is hysterical."

Yes, we were all ready for some light-hearted entertainment. The waiter came by with our check. Stephanie and I went to freshen up while the guys settled it. Before the curtain went up at the theatre, I couldn't help but think that in life, just as in the theatre, we live on a stage with so many stories to tell—some lively, but some dark.

CHAPTER 18

Painful Endings

Seriously, I thought as I hung up the phone. I was expecting some backlash from the layoffs we had to do at our restaurant in Carbondale in southern Illinois, but I never expected to get a call telling me someone had fainted when she heard she was being laid off. The call from Simon, the store manager, was to ask me what they should do.

"Call 911," I'd said as calmly as I could even though I was screaming it to myself. "And once you get her medical help, call me back with an update."

Now, these are highly paid, intelligent people who should have known what to do—call 911 for medical help, not the Corporate Office in Chicago 300 miles away. Despite all the training and preparation we give them—in this case we prepped the regional and store manager and provided scripts to use to deliver the news about the layoff—I still despair at the lack of common sense some people show.

I was still shaking my head in disbelief as I went to the HR conference room for our weekly staff meeting. I must have looked upset because I saw my team looking at each other wondering what now.

"Sorry I'm late, but I was on the phone with Simon in Carbondale. I know you'll think I made this one up, but one of the employees fainted when she got the layoff news, and they called me to find out what to do."

With a casual wave of his hand, Ryan said, "That's why they pay you the big bucks, Maryanne."

My staff knows they can joke with me which is great. It really helps relieve the tension we all feel from time to time. The laughter around the room confirmed they were all comfortable with me and knew they could say what was on their minds.

"I don't think I've ever shared with you something what a mentor told me a long time ago—HR needs to have a five-tissue rule. If it takes more than five tissues to calm an employee down, it's best to ask them to leave and reschedule. I should have shared that with Simon—bet he and his team have used more than a few tissues today."

Kyle, who's usually the one who lightens our moods with a joke or story, was serious this time. "Is the employee all right?"

"I told them to call 911. I haven't heard back, but we probably will shortly."

Gloria Lincoln looked up from the stack of documents in front of her. "I know this may get us off our agenda, and I really hope we can get to the decisions we need to make on open enrollment for our healthcare plan, but I just have to share something that happened in a past life."

I nodded to her to continue. "Unfortunately, I've had to fire a few people in my career. Before I came to work at Kings, I worked in HR at a large medical center. We had an employee who didn't show up for work for a week and didn't call, and we had the typical policy of terminating employment after three days of no show/no call. Imagine my surprise when she actually answered my phone call. I told her she was terminated based on her absence. She screamed that we couldn't fire her, and that she was coming to get me."

"Gloria," Kyle said, "were you frightened?"

"No, I knew we had great security and that I'd be protected, but little did I know what would happen next. She showed up in the lobby and since we'd deactivated her security badge, she had to wait there until I came down. When I got to the lobby, there she was holding a tiny baby in her arms. Another woman was also with her."

"As I walked toward her, she tossed the baby to her friend, came at me and punched me in the jaw."

I gasped. "Gloria, that was awful. Were you hurt? Did the friend catch the baby?"

"Well, I had a split lip and a bruise the size of Chicago on my jaw but thank goodness the friend did catch the baby who was, by this time, screaming at the top of its lungs."

By now everyone was firing questions at Gloria. As she tried to respond, I could tell she was reliving the experience and not in a good way.

"Security grabbed and subdued the woman and took her to the ER for medical assistance. Later, they took her, her baby, and her friend home—I have no idea how they got there. We decided not to press charges, so she wasn't arrested. We never heard from her again, but I learned a valuable lesson—never fire someone over the phone. While I don't know if things would have been different if we'd called her in and done it in person, it's possible we might have avoided the altercation."

"Or, it could have been even worse—what if she'd brought a gun," Ryan exclaimed. "Or she might still have hit you and you wouldn't have had security close by. In a normal termination meeting, you'd have two people but usually not security standing by, right?

"Yes, Ryan's right," I said. "At our last networking meeting, David Morgan, who works at a technology firm told us about a recent situation they had. Someone got really angry with his manager and threatened to kill him—and did it in front of witnesses. The manager went to David and was really frightened. He was concerned that this guy might be serious about the threat and so the firm hired a security company to provide the manager with protection. It was a Friday, and the security firm recommended they stay with the manager 24/7. David thought they'd follow the employee, but they said it was more effective to stick with the manager." I stopped to sip my coffee and that gave my very inquisitive staff time to start asking questions.

"That seems like a bit of overkill—to pay for security when it was just a verbal threat," Gloria said.

Kyle nodded his head in agreement, but it was Noelle Livingston, our Training & Development Director, who spoke up and said, "I think it was probably a good decision, but let's let Maryanne finish the story."

I smiled my thanks to her. "Nothing happened over the weekend, but they kept the security firm in place when they came back to work. David and their legal counsel prepared for a termination. Security was stationed outside David's office, and they'd rehearsed emergency procedures. Turned out the employee was quiet, and very subdued and never even protested his termination—just got up, gathered his stuff, and left quietly and they never heard from him again. It shows how you can never predict what's going to happen. It's always better to be over prepared."

"I remember a time when a line manager and I were terminating a guy for poor performance," Noelle said. "He was an outside sales rep and consistently missed his quarterly quotas. This happened two quarters in a row, and we'd given him all kinds of counseling and support to get him on track. Part of his job was to do a monthly follow up with customers, but we'd heard from several of his very good clients they hadn't seen him for months."

Kyle was sitting back in his chair smiling. "Sounds like it was a pretty straightforward performance issue but I'm guessing since you're sharing it with us it didn't turn out that way."

"You're right," Noelle said laughing. "His manager and I met with him, and the manager outlined the reasons for termination—for the record, he did a really good job of it. He got right to the point and didn't elaborate on the issues. He just outlined where the performance was below standard and told the employee he was being terminated. He probably only spoke for four minutes or so but gave the right information. The employee appeared shocked. Apparently, he didn't take all the counseling and support we'd offered too seriously. He said, 'Please, you have to give me another chance. I didn't want to tell you, but I'm getting a divorce and want to get back in the dating game and I am totally out of shape so I've been spending a lot of time at the health club.'"

Ryan, narrowing his eyes, seemed fixated on Noelle's story. "What does his personal life have to do with him not doing his job? I don't get it."

"I know—seemed mighty strange to me," Noelle continued. "But let me tell you, that manager held his ground. I knew this was difficult for him as he was one of the most empathetic managers I've ever worked with, but he didn't give in. So, the employee tried again to beg for one more chance. He kept saying he'd put in a full day and work out in the evenings rather than at lunch like he'd been doing. He kept digging himself farther in the hole, but the manager was firm in his decision. I did my part by taking care of all the out-processing details. We never found out what happened to him after he left, but we always wondered if he got himself back in shape and found another wife."

I noticed Ryan, the youngest person in our office by far, looking down and squirming in his seat. "I have never told anyone this because I am so embarrassed it happened to me, but I know you guys won't judge me." We looked at each other in great anticipation, exchanging curious glances.

"I had a part time job in college at a very large, upscale apartment complex. I worked in the office on weekends, and it was a great job for a student since most of the time I could study. However, occasionally someone would come in the office and one day a very attractive woman came in wearing a halter top and Daisy Dukes."

"Please tell us more," Kyle said with a smirk.

"Okay but here's the embarrassing part. She leaned over the counter and displayed well, what um, she must have considered her *assets*, placed a stack of cash down, said it was her rent money, practically demanded a receipt—which I would've given her anyway. I'll admit I was totally flustered, and quickly turned back to the desk behind me to get her a receipt. When I turned back to the counter, the cash was gone."

I raised an eyebrow to Kyle who was about to burst into laughter.

"I asked her where it was," Ryan was saying, "and she said I'd taken it with me when I went to get the receipt. I knew I hadn't, but she insisted, grabbed the receipt, and left the office. I was pretty shaken by the experience and called the manager who lived on site. She came to the office and called the police, but when they questioned the woman, she said she'd given me the money and had the receipt to prove it."

"Judging by the fact we're talking terminations here, I am betting you got fired," I said.

"Yes, but not right away. This apartment complex was part of a chain that owned many other apartments in the area, and they were very understanding about what had happened, were going to make some changes, blah, blah. But, about three months later, I was out doing my morning rounds—we were supposed to walk around at least twice on a shift to make sure the park-like setting we had looked pristine—and yes, I am quoting from the sales brochure—when I happened to see the married owner of the company and my manager standing outside the door to her apartment, kissing her like he was saying goodbye—and I mean kissing. I tried to hide but they saw me. I was fired the next day."

Kyle shot up in his chair, no longer finding this funny. "Not because you saw something you shouldn't have," he said.

"No, they actually said it was because of the theft of the rent money. They said their insurance carrier demanded it. At the time, I just wanted to get out of there but now that I've worked with you all, I realize they were skating on thin ice to terminate me on those grounds. I heard recently the owner divorced his wife and married again but not to the manager I worked for. I almost feel badly for her but not really," Ryan said with a smile. "I sure grew up a lot from that experience."

I jumped in and shared one more story. This was one of those really sad situations because we never found out what happened to the individual. This gentleman was hired at the consulting firm I'd worked at right out of college. He was a perfect fit for the job, despite some minor gaps in his employment history. He got along with everyone—genuine nice guy, professional, even-tempered—and did a great job. About nine months later, his manager and director showed up in Jason Edison's office. He hadn't been to work for a week—no call, no show—and they couldn't get in touch with him. Calls were going to voice mail. These were the days before social media and technology dominated communication. He was a valued employee, and his managers wanted to work with him. If he needed a leave, they were fine with that. So, we sent a registered letter to his address.

Ryan was sitting there dumbfounded. I know the concept of limited technology and communication was beyond his comprehension. Gloria was shaking her head and smiling.

"In the letter," I continued, "we expressed concern for his well-being and asked him to contact the firm within five days. He did call Jason who explained we wanted to work with him—give him a leave if necessary—but needed to know what was going on and when we could expect him back. He was grateful but told Jason he couldn't tell him anything other than he wasn't in danger. At that point, Jason told him we'd hold his job for a week. When he didn't return or contact us, we considered him a voluntary termination for job abandonment. We sent his out-processing paperwork along with the few personal items he'd left behind to his last-known address and never heard anything further from him."

"Couldn't you have tracked him down somehow?" asked Ryan.

"The firm had done all they could. This was a real-life cliffhanger, and it was painful for everyone. His manager had shared the employee had been through a contentious divorce and custody battle. We could only speculate whether or not that had something to do with his disappearance. Had he kidnapped the son? Was he in jail? Were the gaps in his employment somehow related? All this dark speculation was so out of character for this very personable and professional guy."

Just then my cell rang, and it was Simon in Carbondale. I asked if it was okay to put him on speaker, since we were in the HR Department staff meeting. He agreed. "We got her to the hospital and she's fine. She is totally embarrassed at her reaction, but she admitted she'd skipped breakfast this morning. They checked her out at the ER, and I dropped her off at home on my way back to the restaurant."

"Thanks, Simon. We're all pleased she is all right. I assume we will need to follow up with her to give her the rest of the information you were sharing with those who were being laid off," said Gloria—ever the benefits manager she is.

"Yes, Gloria, can you give her a call later and fill her in?"

"Email me the details and I will get with her as soon as we finish here." Gloria said.

I disconnected the call, and we moved on with our agenda. Talking about the benefits open enrollment details seemed pretty tame after this discussion.

CHAPTER 19

Just When You Thought You'd Heard It All

Jason Edison, oblivious to Linda and David who were bringing in the snacks, was sitting at his usual spot at the head of the table fiddling with his phone. This was so uncharacteristic for him. He's always so attentive to everything and everyone around him. Looking up, he shook his head in disbelief. "You've got to hear this one." Everyone turned to look at him.

"I just received this email from one of our consultants. He's been working at a client's building in an office park with a number of ponds which are attracting quite a large population of Canadian geese. Apparently, despite signs from the building management stating *Please Don't Feed the Geese*, employees are doing it anyway, making the geese more aggressive—following employees from their cars to the door of the building looking for food. Some employees are so intimidated, they're afraid to get out of their cars. This has created a feud, of sorts, between employees who feed them and the other employees who consider them pests and want them gone."

Thrusting out his chest, David Morgan turned to him with an air of feigned authority. "I'm pretty sure they are Canada geese—not Canadian."

"Such a stickler for details," laughed Jason with a big grin on his face. "Anyway, yesterday morning employees were congregating around the building on their way into work gawking at a goose walking around …" He stopped to clear his throat, "walking around with an arrow through its head."

The look on Stephanie Packard's face caused the rest of us in the room to erupt into laughter. "Wait, what?" she said trying to compose herself. "The goose was shot in the head with an arrow and was still walking around?"

"That's what I said," Jason replied, trying not to totally lose it. "And now the geese-feeding employees are in an uproar. They think someone on the night shift—a known bow hunter—shot the goose and are *demanding* he be fired. And they are protesting because the property management company wants to call the game warden to remove, and likely euthanize, the goose. Instead, they want to call a rescue team and take a collection to help it recover."

David, who was sitting back taking this all in, now leaned forward. "And what about the other employees? The ones who can't get out of their cars? Are they taking up a collection to buy more arrows for the hunter?" At this point, everyone was laughing.

Stephanie could hardly get her words out. "I still can't get the image of the goose calmly walking around with an arrow through *its head* out of *my head.*"

"I hate to say this," said Linda Goodman, "but I do understand where this bow hunter may be coming from. These geese can be aggressive and problematic. Did anyone see the article in the paper last week about the pedestrian who was bitten by one in a bus parking lot? The rescuers thought the goose felt threatened by the street noise and bit the poor pedestrian in response. Fortunately for the pedestrian, the injuries weren't life-threatening."

"Jason, any idea what the company's going to do?" I said reaching for a napkin.

"The second message I received said the building management company is agreeing to call a rescue organization and let the employees make a donation to help the injured goose," Jason replied. "But the bigger problem appears to be the constant feeding of the geese. As Linda pointed out, they aren't always tame. There needs to be a stronger message sent to the employees about the dangers of feeding the geese."

"What is wrong with people," I said. "You've got a group of employees ignoring, no defying, a request, no a directive, from property management and adding to a problem situation. Yet they think they can demand someone be fired."

"Oh, the issues we get involved in. No one ever told me I'd have to be a zoo-keeper when I went into human resources," Ellen Cooper said. "But this reminds me of another animal story I once heard from a colleague." She went on to tell us about an employee who felt she hit something driving to work. From her rearview window, she saw a squirrel lying in the road, and it appeared to be moving. She pulled onto the shoulder of the road, parked her car, walked to where the squirrel was laying, and attempted to move it off the road. The squirrel reciprocated by biting her. She had the good sense to leave it there and drive to the urgent care center near her office, but not before calling animal control to report it.

"When she got into work, two hours late, she explained what happened and asked to file a worker's compensation claim, because she was on her way to work when this happened so naturally her injury was work related."

"Did HR file the claim?" I asked.

"They most certainly did…" Ellen paused, "Not."

"When they refused, explaining commuting time was not work time so the company wasn't responsible, she complained to the State Workers' Compensation Board. Guess what they told her? The same thing. Apparently, the injury was minor—she wasn't bitten that hard— and she really didn't suffer any loss, except the co-payment for the medical visit."

"It never ceases to amaze me what people do," said Jason. "Why do their bad decisions—personal decisions—somehow become their employer's responsibility?"

Stephanie, who appeared to be deep in thought, suddenly turned in my direction. I couldn't help noticing the glint in her eyes. "Speaking of workers' comp claims, you all know my husband Norm worked in manufacturing for most of his career. He had a doozy of a situation once. As a new manager for the facilities department, the machine shop also reported to him. Well, about a month into this new role, two women claimed a male coworker was sexually harassing them. The guy was a big, burly person, I think an ex-Marine. Their male HR manager was on vacation, so two women from another plant were sent to investigate. While they were interviewing the man, he got very agitated— apparently this was the first time he heard the specific allegations. He stood up, towering over them, and said 'I'll be right back. Stay right here. Don't move.' And, he ran from the room."

She stopped to take a sip of coffee. "By this time, the women were paralyzed with fear, but one of them spotted a phone in the conference room where they were sitting. She dialed Norm's office extension, but he was out on the floor. So, she left a message. Just then the man returned waving a 6-inch cylindrical piece of metal and said, 'See this?' as he shoved it in their faces. They both nodded, too shaken to say anything. 'Relax,' he said, 'I'm not going to hurt you.' Then he explained one of the two women who'd filed the complaint crafted the metal piece into a crude phallic symbol and had been chasing men around the shop with it for the past several months."

Linda raised her hand. "Whoa. Where was Norm during all of this? And what does this have to do with workers' comp?"

"I'm getting there," said Stephanie. "About this time, Norm heard the message, detected fear in the woman's voice, and rushed to the conference room where he was quickly brought up to date. Remember, Norm had only been the manager for a few weeks and the pipe-wielding culprit had apparently toned it down a bit, probably waiting to get a handle on the new boss. But that wasn't it. *Mr. Burly* found the pipe in a drawer in the shop and confiscated it. Norm stayed while they finished the interview, then he and the women walked to HR and requested to see the pipe-wielding culprit's file. They also wanted to know if there was any other information about her that might be pertinent. The HR staff member, who was fairly young, asked if the workers' comp claim she filed had any relevance to the case. Well, it did. She filed the claim about four or five months earlier because she'd gotten metal shavings embedded in her skin—right around the time she'd crafted her *masterpiece*."

As Stephanie took a pause, Linda interjected. "I'm surprised no one made a connection between her *masterpiece,* as you put it Stephanie, and her injury. Someone should have asked her what she was doing when the injury occurred."

"Apparently, the occupational nurse who took care of workers' comp was new to the job and still learning about the company," Stephanie said.

The investigation took a different direction at that point, focusing on this new culprit. *Mr. Burly* was counseled about the course language he sometime used, especially when he was being chased—which was the basis of the harassment charge. And the woman who was wielding the pipe was given a stern written warning about her behavior, including doing non-authorized metal work in the shop, misuse of company equipment and resources, sexually harassing her male co-workers, and possibly a safety violation. The other woman also received a disciplinary notice, which she claimed was unfair, even though she'd helped make the objectionable pipe and cheered her coworker on when she chased the men.

I'd been unconsciously fumbling with my bracelet. "Stephanie, I find it curious they sent two women to conduct the sexual harassment investigation. Couldn't they have sent a man and a woman, especially since the two women claimed they felt physically threatened by this big, burly guy? At a minimum, Norm could have been present during the interviews, as a witness."

As everyone's heads were nodding, Stephanie said, "Norm had the same reaction at the time and said something to the plant's HR manager when he got back from vacation. The decision about the investigations was made by the District HR Manager—someone light on employee relations experience. The women complained directly to him, and he panicked, assuming they were being straight with him and believing every word they said on face value. Never considered there could be more to the situation and didn't know anyone involved. He wanted to move quickly, likely planning to fire *Mr. Burly*. Of course, nothing got resolved until the plant's HR manager returned the following week. And poor Norm had to deal with all this tension in the shop in the meantime."

"There are so many facets to HR. People just don't realize it. You know, at times I believe some people think we sit around HR drinking coffee, waiting for them to bring us their problem of the day. How absurd is that? But I bet I can top Norm's story," said Linda tapping her beautifully manicured fingernails on the table.

All eyes were on her, waiting for her to continue. I know I wasn't the only one wondering if things could get any more bizarre. And, of course, they did.

"You all know I've spent most of my career in the hospitality industry, including hotels. At one of the hotels, we had a number of female employees from Central American countries, and a U.S.-born coworker complained about two of them. Apparently, one had an eye infection, and they both believed breast milk had healing properties. Turns out, the other one was nursing, so the one with the infection asked her lactating friend to help her out. One morning in the locker room she laid down on a bench while the other woman pulled out her breast and squirted milk directly into her infected eye."

"Oh, stop," said Ellen as she burst into laughter. "Did anyone see them?"

"Obviously, yes," said Linda. "That's how we found out about it. It was the beginning of a shift change, and there were a number of women in the locker room."

David, who'd gotten up to stretch as Linda started talking, was now laughing so hard, he was sliding down the wall. And then I noticed Jason, looking at his phone, again. "Wait," he said. "I just Googled healing properties for breast milk."

"Does it say anything about eye infections?" Linda asked.

"As a matter of fact, it does. Mothers have often used breast milk to treat conjunctivitis. It's proven to be the most effective liquid to treat babies and children with the eye infection. Use an eyedropper to apply two drops into the infected eye, and it will get rid of the infection in a jiffy. Tip, it can also be used as a contact lens solution for cleansing."

"Do you think they were using it instead of saline solution?" I asked. "Are there any other good tips?"

"Yes, there are," said Jason, using his gruffest voice to sound authoritative. "It also says breast milk can be a cost-effective solution for acne or as a facial cleanser. The breast milk should be applied over the entire face then wiped away clean with a towel."

"Please. Don't put any more images in my head tonight, Jason," said Stephanie.

"You know, we couldn't make this stuff up even if we tried," I said. "No joking, what happened to the women?"

"The person who complained claimed it was sexual harassment— she shouldn't have had to be subjected to that scene nor to another woman's bare breast. So, we investigated it and talked to others who were witnesses—none of whom were bothered by it. In fact, most of them weren't paying attention and hadn't noticed it. When we spoke to the two women, they were totally confused. They didn't see anything wrong in their actions. This was perfectly common in their country. We explained how our customs differed, and they should have been more discreet. We put them on notice not to do this in the future. The complaining party wanted them both fired—another example how some employees think they can decide the outcome. In fact, she was so upset when we didn't fire the women, she quit. The incident did start a company-wide discussion about providing lactation rooms which we ultimately did."

"Since we have a pattern going here, I must ask, did the eye infection clear up or did it get worse and was a workers' comp claim filed?" Jason inquired.

"You sure have been in rare form tonight, Mr. Edison," Linda said.

"Laughter does relieve stress and goodness knows we all need that relief from time to time," he replied.

"People and their issues can wear you down," Linda said. "People don't realize the intensity of some of the situations we encounter in human resources."

"Well, just when you thought you heard it all, someone comes along with yet another peculiar situation. We are so fortunate to have this group. And a safe, confidential environment to exchange challenges and ideas," I said. "Most of you know I've been informally mentoring this young woman, Allison. When I first met her, she asked me how you learn employee relations."

"Slowly and painfully—with practice and experience," said Jason.

"Exactly," I replied. "We all made mistakes and needed guidance early in our careers. What would you think if we expanded this group and brought in some young professionals, perhaps every other month?"

"Great way to give back, but how would we structure it? Same informal format?" asked Stephanie. "And what would we talk about?"

"Ah, all the shades of grey," I sighed.

Jason jumped in, "There really is no black and white in our work."

I looked around the table at my valued colleagues, smiled and said, "And, we have so many more stories to tell."

Acknowledgements

Writing this book was both a joy and a challenge. One of the joys came from the amazing cooperation we received from friends and colleagues when we asked for their unbelievable tales from the workplace. Everyone had great stories to share, but that's where we met one of the challenges—keeping the people and their organizations confidential.

So, we'd like to express our gratitude to everyone who shared stories with us, and you know who you are. We'll thank you all personally, privately, and profusely.

All of the other books we've written are nonfiction. This book is in a new genre, creative nonfiction. We took real work experiences from real people and created new stories. So, another challenge was to learn new skills—storytelling and writing dialogue and a lot more.

We're grateful to the generous writers who taught us new skills, shared tips, and revealed that every good writer does multiple revisions and rewrites. We're thankful for the professionals at Writers Digest for their annual conference which allowed us to meet and learn from great writers and publishing professionals while hanging out in New York City and visiting our favorite Barnes & Noble store on Fifth Avenue. It was there that we met the fabulous Cal Hunt who manages the business book department, and who gave our books wonderful exposure.

Along the way on our journey of writing this book we had tremendous support starting with Lisa Barrow. We reached out to her early in the process as we began to put this book idea together. She worked with us as a developmental editor during many different stages of writing this book, and her advice was invaluable. We owe a debt of gratitude to the people who took their time to read and review the manuscript. Special thanks to them, including Ilene Colina, Jan Maples, June O'Dell Porco, Judy Perault, Mando Lara, James Stevens, Joe Cardillo, Jean Waterman, and Kit Crumpton. Your feedback was priceless.

There were also people who gave us encouragement. Thanks to our colleagues and friends from our business book club in Virginia who've been there for us over the years we spent writing this book: Alice Waagen, Judy Perrault, Linda Keller, Lynn Lorenz, Marsha Hughes-Rease, Mary Tack, Mary Lou Byrne, Mary Walter Arthur, and Sarah Rajtik. A special shout-out to Cornelia's writing colleagues in New Mexico who provided valuable insights toward the end of this journey: Heloise Jones, Paul Shank, Jane Bardal, Hana Norton, and Jane Epstein.

Our wonderful literary agent, Marilyn Allen of the Allen O'Shea Agency, continues to encourage and inspire us every step of the way. Thanks for always being there when we need you.

Susan Devereaux provided her excellent editing and proofreading skills and helped us improve the stories we tell. Thanks for your professionalism and your friendship.

Erik Gamlem has kept our social media efforts on track, always assuring that our blogs and tweets are posted, and that all our platforms, especially LinkedIn, are up to date.